# THE
# CHALLENGE
# OF
# AGING

## A Bibliography

Compiled by
MARGARET E. MONROE
and
RHEA JOYCE RUBIN

LIBRARIES UNLIMITED, INC.                    1983
Littleton, Colorado

LIBRARIES UNLIMITED, INC.
P.O. Box 263
Littleton, Colorado 80160-0263

---

**Library of Congress Cataloging in Publication Data**

Monroe, Margaret Ellen, 1914-
    The challenge of aging.

    Includes index.
    1. Aged--Bibliography.  2. Aging--Bibliography.
I. Rubin, Rhea Joyce.  II. Title.
Z7164.04M66  1983  [HQ1061]      016.3052'6      83-7942
ISBN 0-87287-387-0

Libraries Unlimited books are bound with Type II nonwoven material
that meets and exceeds National Association of State Textbook
Administrators' Type II nonwoven material specifications Class A
through E.

This book is dedicated to ...

Those librarians and student librarians who
shared our efforts to bring books to all who face
the lifetasks of aging

and

those who use books and other library resources
because they find that reading prepares for
living.

# TABLE
# OF
# CONTENTS

## TASKS OF ADJUSTMENT (cont'd)

## TASKS OF MAJOR CHANGE

## TASKS OF OPPORTUNITY

# ACKNOWLEDGMENTS

This bibliography has evolved from its beginnings in 1975-1976 in a special year's program of advanced study in library service to aging at the University of Wisconsin—Madison. This program with its interest in literature on aging continued through four years of financial support from the Faye McBeath Institute on Aging and Adult Life for the preparation of experienced public librarians in service to older adults. During this period (1975-1979) the lifetasks concept evolved and a basic pool of evaluated books was established. Grateful acknowledgment goes to Dr. Martin B. Loeb, then Director, and to Dr. Vivian I. Wood, then Associate Director, Faye McBeath Institute, for their support of this instructional program, its related research, and the spin-off in this bibliography. Dr. Wood's interest extended to reading and advising on the final draft of the bibliography; her aid was of special value in points of emphasis in gerontology and in the philosophy of aging.

The students in the 1975-1976 eleven-month program of advanced study in library service to aging did the preliminary work of book identification and organization of the selected titles by lifetask. Special recognition goes to Carolyn Wilson, Elizabeth Anslow, and Judith Clark for their establishment of the pool of titles from which this bibliography has evolved. The significant work of 38 later students in identifying new task definitions and titles relevant to the task list is here acknowledged, with identification of the work of special value from Rhonda Gandel, Nancy Bolin, Jean Ford, Robert Rapp, Sari Feldman, Bill Wilson, and Joyce Mitchell. The work of Louise Schmidt in developing the concept of spiritual well-being as a lifetask is warmly acknowledged. Quite special thanks to three "older adult" friends who gave three hours one afternoon to critiquing the lifetask list, confirming its reality, and suggesting their priorities within it: Florence Blake, Katherine Kaseman, and Mildred Kreager. The task of keeping order in the evolving pool of titles from which these in the bibliography were partly selected fell to three student assistants whose eager, competent, informed help was crucial, and the thanks of the senior author go gratefully to Allison Landers, Rhonda Gandel, and Debra Spear.

As plans for this bibliography itself formally developed, Rhea Joyce Rubin joined Margaret E. Monroe to share in its authorship by taking responsibility for the final shaping of the "creative literature" sections of the list. The collaborative authorship has happily survived the pressures of major research projects, one retirement, one birth, and other acts of God and of professional careers.

The two authors wish to acknowledge with gratitude the help of families, friends, and colleagues in suggestions of book titles and comments on concepts and drafts of the manuscript. Especially valuable has been the interest of three persons: Joan Sullivan, Outreach Librarian to Older Adults, Dane County Library Services, who supplied books, suggested titles, and talked things over; Dr. Elliott E. Kanner, Resources Coordinator, North Suburban (Wheeling, Illinois) Library System, who dedicated hours of time from January through March, 1982, to title identification, evaluation, and supplying copies for analysis by the senior author; Orrilla T. Blackshear, retired Assistant Director, Madison Public Library, whose depth and breadth of reading and seasoned book judgment were brought to bear both in the early stages and in the final preparation to the great benefit of the bibliography.

For assistance in checking bibliographic detail, our thanks to Kathy Scott (in California) and to Anna Mae Prem (in Wisconsin). For supply of materials needed for book analysis, thanks to Chris Jocius in Illinois and to the staff of the Madison Public Library in Wisconsin. Rhea J. Rubin extends special thanks to Lawrence Berman for his patience and to their daughter Hannah for much diversion.

Never more truly has it been said that while these sources of help may be credited with many of whatever excellences may be found in this bibliography, whatever inadequacies are found in the structure of the list or in the selection and annotation of the items are purely the responsibility of the authors. We shall hope to receive criticisms and suggestions so that later editions may benefit by the continued pooling of wisdom!

Margaret E. Monroe
Rhea Joyce Rubin

# HOW TO
# USE
# THIS BOOK

---

This is a bibliography, an annotated reading list of nontechnical books for the layperson, grouped around lifetasks that older adults will confront as they move from middle years to retirement and to older age. These are tasks of major change (such as widowhood, grief, social isolation, dying), tasks of adjustment (such as retirement, new lifestyles, life review, changes in health), and tasks of opportunity (such as leisure, self-actualization, perspective building). Each lifetask is introduced with a description of the aspects of the task itself, which is followed by a list of the readings related to that task. The books in each lifetask section are presented in a logical sequence, rather than an alphabetical sequence, to enable reading the bibliography as if reading an ordinary book. Each title is indexed by author, title, and subject at the end of the bibliography, so that it is simple to locate a particular book in the one, two, or more places where it is used in the list.

Thus, it becomes clear that the authors envision two quite different kinds of use to which this reading list will be put. First, it is designed to provide an overview of the experience of aging for the older adult, or for a person who looks ahead to understand the aging experience. Here the introductions to each lifetask section are of prime importance, and the annotations of the books amplify and illustrate the ideas in the introductions when they are read in sequence following the introductions.

The second kind of use is as a tool to help in selection of books on a particular subject in the area of the experience of aging. Here the table of contents and the index provide the approaches to the titles to be considered; the selection of particular titles is aided by the annotations for individual books.

In addition to these two uses of the bibliography by readers and by librarians serving readers, there is the use that social gerontologists and activity directors in senior centers and community centers may make in selecting reading materials for group programs, group therapy, and group discussion. Book titles supplementary to a main entry are clustered within the annotation for the main entry title, each one of which, however, is listed in the index by title, author, and subject. Further, materials especially good for group use are so identified in the annotation, and when brief sections of books seem suitable for use with groups with specific interests, the chapter or pages are identified.

The bibliographic entry focuses on title, which the layperson's literature on aging invites. Author, publisher, date, pages, and price follow. Hardcover editions precede paperbound editions, which are followed by large type edition information. Prices are included when books were found to be in print in fall 1982; if price is omitted the book was out of print but is widely available in public libraries. The omission of publisher, date, and pages—as in the case of Robert Browning's "Rabbi Ben Ezra"—indicates that the poem is widely available in various editions of Browning's collected poetry or in anthologies; librarians will have no problem in locating copies.

Following each annotation there is a listing of the Library of Congress code numbers by which nonprint formats of the reading may be ordered from the National Library Service (NLS) for the Blind and Physically Handicapped. Although use of these formats is restricted to those enrolled in the NLS, a division of the Library of Congress, enrollment is a simple process through local public libraries for those who qualify by reason of visual impairment (permanent or temporary), physical handicap, or reading disability.

| | |
|---|---|
| Currently Recorded Formats: | Recorded Disc (RD) |
| | Recorded Cassette (RC) |
| Discontinued But Still | |
| Available Formats: | Braille (BR or BRA) |
| | Cassette Book (CB) |
| | Talking Book (TB) |

Other code numbers tend to be locally produced but nationally available materials and serve as order numbers. Any questions about these materials and their availability or the machinery for playing them will be readily answered by any area Regional Library for the Blind and Physically Handicapped, or by a call to their national offices at (202) 882-5500.

Stories, plays, poems, and books that have been made into 35mm commercial films are specifically noted; production information for the films is given. Original films dealing with the tasks of aging are not listed. If film is available in 16mm form only, it is so indicated. Readers interested in additional films on aging should consult the most complete guide available:

*About Aging: A Catalog of Films*
Mildred V. Allyn, ed.
Los Angeles: Univ. of Southern California
Andrus Gerontology Center
4th edition, 1979. Supplement, 1981.

# AGING
# AS
# OPPORTUNITY

---

"Life is a banquet, and most people starve to death."

— Anonymous

Affluence, medical advances, social policy, and new technologies have combined to provide significantly greater time to live for a large proportion of people in the American society. Old age has been postponed from the sixties to the eighties for many. A new major stage of life has been added to peak-of-career and retirement stages for many in the professions, management, and skilled trades, and most of this new phase relates not to earning a living but to the art of living. Aging has become for many a period of opportunity.

The readings proposed in this bibliography have been selected not only for those currently experiencing aging but also for those who wisely look ahead and who will use the decade or two before their sixties arrive to adjust perspectives and to rehearse the new roles that aging provides in our society. These readings have been grouped by the lifetasks to which their authors speak.

Aging is a life stage that brings with it new tasks that must be performed successfully to assure happy older years: tasks of major change, tasks of adjustment, tasks of meeting new opportunities. All require learning, new insights, change, growth. The people we are at

60 need not be the people we are at 80. The experiences of new roles in family and community, living with death and the process of grief, the enrichment of our later years' life review, and the arts of leisure and creative fulfillment can bring an expanded identity, a fresh self-awareness that makes aging a rich affirmation of our lives.[1]

There are some people who have experienced aging as opportunity for growth and "becoming," people who know the later years to be fulfilling. Reading in and around these lifetasks, both in fiction and creative literature as well as in nonfiction and more formal explication of these tasks, is useful as we look ahead to these years and as we experience them in daily life. Those in their forties may find rehearsal of the tasks of the sixties important to do now; those in their sixties may do well to look ahead to the eighties. Reading provides both the orientation that allows us not to be taken completely by surprise and thus prevents or softens crises, and also provides the rich resource to which we instinctively turn back when a crisis is upon us.

Reading is a personal matter, as is all experience. Yet shared reading (reading with discussion or reading aloud) brings added useful reflection on the author's perspective and enables the unfamiliar or the confronting idea to be more understandable. The selections here are often identified for their special usefulness in shared reading.

The reading selections are grouped by lifetask, and when a volume is particularly important to more than one lifetask it will be included in a second or third entry. The index will help you locate these "added entries." The table of contents guides you to the organization of this book. A brief introduction to each lifetask precedes the readings around that task.

---

[1]Detailed discussion of the "lifetask" concept under the term "developmental tasks" is available in Robert Havighurst's *Developmental Tasks and Education*, 3d ed. (New York: David McKay, 1972), pp. 108-109; and in Lillian R. Dangott and Richard A. Kalish's *A Time to Enjoy: The Pleasures of Aging* (Englewood Cliffs, N.J.: Prentice-Hall, 1978), pp. 112-37.

# TASKS
# OF
# ADJUSTMENT

---

Not since adolescence have we been required in our society to make as dramatic and numerous changes as we are asked to do in our mid-sixties. New relations to our families, our jobs, and our communities are thrust upon us, taxing our mature balance, flexibility, and self-image. Those who bridge these role changes successfully have a good chance for happy later years. Retirement for many men and women is the first unavoidable challenge to change, and often requires the creation of a new identity to sustain self-esteem. Out of the new image of aging for our society has come a sound basis for acceptance of the after-work life, of a new role with spouse and with one's adult children and their families, of a new role for friendship. Concerns with physical and mental health are essential in this transitional stage, and such practical matters as income and housing require adequate solution if the "good life" is to be attainable. Many of these matters need planning and "rehearsal" if the major task of adjustment is to be accomplished.

## NEW IMAGE OF AGING

The new and positive image of aging will take on reality in our society only as older adults, in their attitudes and behavior, demonstrate flexibility, capacity for intellectual curiosity, wisdom in human relations, and perception of older age as a time for growth, contribution, and enjoyment.

The new image of aging is emerging not only in the books listed in this section as creations of their authors but also in the lives of people the authors cite and describe. A wealth of new "role models" are emerging: the hobbyist, the political activist, the elder counselor, the generation-gap bridger, the family time-binder, and on and on. Dominantly, however, the new image of aging focuses on unashamed acceptance of being old and recognition of old age as offering a new stage of life fulfillment.

A chief barrier to older adults' new self-image is the reluctance of the not-yet-old population to adopt this view of aging. While long-term self-interest might argue that all society should perceive old age as an acceptable and honorable stage of life, tradition and immediate self-interest spur the young to the conscious or unconscious "put-down" of the older adult. Competition for jobs, for roles of power in the family, for leadership in the neighborhood and community have made it a useful tradition for young and middle-aged adults to edge out the older adult. The "new" older adult may adopt an assertiveness in claiming rightful roles in family, community, economic, and political life. At the same time, the necessity of allowing appropriate adult roles of leadership and power for the middle-aged and the young adult places reasonable limits on the older person's grasp of familiar roles. This dilemma is centuries-old, and only goodwill and creative collaboration among generations can find solutions for each new era.

Reading, reflection, and discussion of the varied new images of aging provide a useful beginning to preparation for this stage of life. In a very real sense, the older adult who is in the sixties or seventies in the United States represents a wholly new generation of relatively healthy, educated, leisured adults, and the new image of this generation is just now in the making.


**Why Survive? Being Old in America.** Robert N. Butler. New York: Harper & Row, 1975. 512p. $19.95; Paper 1977. $5.95.

This comprehensive survey for the layman of what being old in America meant in the mid-1970s gave impetus to many reforms now under way, but the combination of careful factual presentation on the many aspects of older adult life (housing, income, health, and so forth) with the angry rejection of the status quo for this rapidly growing population makes this a continuingly important book. Butler headed the National Institute on Aging during the late 1970s; the book was the basis for his receiving the Pulitzer Prize in 1975.

**Elders in Rebellion: A Guide to Senior Activism.** Louis M. Cottin. Garden City, N.Y.: Doubleday/Anchor Press, 1979. 224p. $8.95.

A skilled journalist and dedicated elder rebel, Cottin reviews the action needed in solving problems in health, housing, retirement, crime, and the public image of older adults in America. He sets forth volunteerism, senior centers, and public welfare programs with clear-eyed analysis of how they help and how they limit the lives of elders. Cottin advises on the action older adults, alone or in groups or organizations, can take to create a reasonable life in the third phase of living.

**Thirty Dirty Lies about Old.** Hugh Downs. San Francisco: Argus Communications, 1979. 181p. $9.95; Paper $2.95; Large Type, Boston: G. K. Hall, 1979.

Thirty negative or limiting stereotypes about aging ("older people want to be young," "intelligence declines with age," "old people are eccentric," "it's bad to dwell on the past," "old people have no interest in sex," etc.) are given highly informed comment in informal style. Each comment, of one to three pages in length, offers a fine basis for discussion of new perspectives on aging. Easy reading, informative, discussable for almost everyone from 15 to 95.

**A Good Age.** Alex Comfort. New York: Crown Publishers, 1976. 224p. $9.95; Paper. New York: Simon & Schuster, 1978. $5.95.

Humane, tough-minded, informed, Comfort presents a definition of terms (from *ageism* to *youth!*) that compose his comments on aging as a social fact that need not be dreaded once we recognize that biological aging need not mean social death. Comfort's comments on any one of his terms (*arthritis, memory, wrinkles*) offer a good basis for reflection and discussion. Readable, relaxed.

**The Aging Game: Success, Sanity, and Sex after Sixty.** Barbara Gallatin Anderson. New York: McGraw-Hill, 1979. 240p. $12.95; Paper 1981. $4.45.

"You can win the aging game but ...," says Anderson, successful aging requires strategy. Anderson's strategies include self-acceptance, acceptance of the later years, replacing lost satisfactions, development of resources and human alliances. Alertness, action, and involvement are her theme. Good anecdotes and shared experiences worth reflecting on and discussing.

**Strategies for the Second Half of Life.** Peter Weaver. New York: Franklin Watts, 1980. 394p. $12.95; Paper. New York: New American Library/Signet, 1981. $3.50.

Brief, practical essays clustered around money management, health, happiness (in friends, love, and activity), family, and perspectives on aging and death. Subtitled "Not a Retirement Book," this has highly readable, well-captioned short chapters followed by a list of resources and readings. This useful "manual" format echoes comparable books such as *The Best Years Catalogue* by Leonard Biegel (New York: G. P. Putnam's Sons, 1978).

**Second Chance: Blueprints for Life Change.** Herbert B. Livesey. Philadelphia: J. B. Lippincott, 1977. 238p.

Brief biographical sketches of a great diversity of people who saw the second chance and took it, even late in life. Anecdotal, readable, discussable. One more of the "strategy" books.

**A Time to Enjoy: The Pleasures of Aging.** Lillian R. Dangott and Richard A. Kalish. Englewood Cliffs, N.J.: Prentice-Hall, 1978. 182p. $11.95; Paper $4.95.

Challenging the past stereotypes of aging, Dangott and Kalish focus on aging as a life-stage for self-actualization. Documenting their perspectives from the thinking of other social gerontologists, they also include useful guides to exercise, diet, relief of stress, biofeedback, and the psychodynamics of health. The brief sections on grief and mourning and on death are excellent. The final chapter, "The Pleasures of Aging," is the unique contribution of this book: leisure, "pleasuring," and personal fulfillment in older age.

**These Rich Years: A Journal of Retirement.** Jean and Robert Hersey. New York: Charles Scribner and Sons, 1969. 270p.

A just-retired professional couple reflect (each in alternating chapters) on what retirement means, its adjustments and opportunities. The ambience of relaxed leisure spiced with adventure and moments of daring is projected as that of the new image of aging. The newly warm relationship developed (and occasionally negotiated) between the retired couple offers an especially significant insight.

BR 01516

**The Measure of My Days.** Florida Scott-Maxwell. New York: Alfred A. Knopf, 1968. 150p.; Paper. New York: Penguin Books, 1979. $2.95.

Reflections on aging, its special perspectives, opportunities, and limitations. This diary, kept when the author was in her mid-eighties and vigorous in mind if not always in body, provides flashback insights into her life of homemaking, work for women's suffrage, writing, and work as a psychoanalyst (a career she began in her forties). Penetrating insights and warm human perceptions about what it means to be old.

**After Ninety.** Imogen Cunningham. Seattle: University of Washington Press, 1977. 112p. $20; Paper $10.95.

Absolutely fascinating faces of people over 90 who were still vital and functioning people. These are not the faces generally seen in nursing homes. These exemplify the new image of aging for the "old old."

**The Art of Aging.** Evelyn Mandel. Edited by Miriam Frost. Minneapolis: Winston Press, 1981. 176p. $14.95; Paper $8.95.

Body (simple exercises and advice on diet), Spirit (some beautiful faces interpreted by lines of poetry), and Mind (13 brief profiles providing role models for aging) are seen by Evelyn Mandel as the key to the art of aging. A book to live with as well as to read and reflect on with others. Here indeed is the new image of aging.

## Creative Literature

**"Rabbi Ben Ezra."** Robert Browning.

"Grow old along with me/The best is yet to be" opens this famous poem on the joys and tasks of aging. Browning at his vigorous, inscrutable best, brings modern insights to his Victorian world. Available in a multitude of collections.

TB 04537

**"Beautiful Old Age."** D. H. Lawrence. In his *Selected Poems.* New York: Penguin Books, 1980. $3.50.

"It ought to be lovely to be old...." Lawrence urges younger people to look to old age as an example and to be unafraid of their own aging.

**Man on the Mountain.** Gladys Hasty Carroll. Boston: Little, Brown and Company, 1969. 223p.

In the twenty-first century, a vast imaginary continent called Great Country is divided into four states; citizens are segregated by age. Two boys, Dunwoodie Keogh and Chuck Ryan, run away from their homes in Two State and end up in Old State, where only people over 60 live. The oldsters refuse to let them return home unless two oldsters are allowed to tour the other states. Religious and didactic in tone, the novel is nevertheless interesting, and the loneliness of old people and of children in such a society is well depicted.

**The Tragedy of the Elderly Gentleman.** George Bernard Shaw. In his *Back to Methuselah: A Metabiological Pentateuch*, pp. 157-231. New York: Brentanos, 1921; Paper. New York: Penguin Books, 1972. $2.95.

Part 4 of the *Pentateuch*, this three-act play set in Ireland in 3000 A.D., deals with the concepts of age and old age. Act 1 (pp. 157-97) has an elderly gentleman visiting from England, the capitol of which is Baghdad. He talks with natives of this land who live to be 300 years old and who refer to people like him as "shortlivers." Shaw uses this scenario to make comments on science, on Irish-British relations, on war, and on age. Perhaps the most provocative is presented by Zoo (p. 183): "But it is not the number of years we have behind us, but the number we have before us, that makes us careful and responsible.... If I knew I had to die in 20 years it would not be worth my while to educate myself. I should not bother about anything but having a little pleasure while I lasted." The play has much to feed a discussion on age and its responsibilities.

BR 01378; RC 16326

**The American Dream.** Edward Albee. New York: Coward-McCann, Inc., 1960; Paper. New York: Coward-McCann and Geoghegan, Inc., 1961. 93p. $3.75.

An absurd play about a family and their (America's) values. Grandma does all the work for Mommy and Daddy, who threaten her with the "van man" to take her away if she doesn't cooperate. In the preface, Albee asks, "Is the play offensive? I certainly hope so; it was my intention to offend as well as to amuse and entertain. Is it nihilistic, immoral, defeatist? ... it is a picture of our time." This is a longer version of an earlier play entitled *The Sandbox*. The new image of aging is projected in the minds of the readers not through what is said or seen but through what Albee's skillful satire stimulates in the minds of the viewers.

**They.** Marya Mannes. Garden City, N.Y.: Doubleday and Company, 1968. 215p.

A society of the future is depicted in the journal of an old person who chronicles her life and four others' lives. All old people, these five live in segregated communities and have no access to the other worlds;

they never meet their grandchildren, and they face mandatory retirement at 50 and mandatory euthanasia at 65. The problems with "they" (the young) started after World War II with adoration of youth and dismissal of history. The five oldsters discuss this and other historical/philosophical issues. The prologue and epilogue reveal that the manuscript, which was recovered from their burning house during their group suicide, has become a popular item on college campuses in society where the only print materials are underground publications.

**A Generation Removed.** Gary K. Wolf. Garden City, N.Y.: Doubleday and Company, 1977. 188p.

An exciting, albeit violent, satiric novel in the futuristic mode about the "Gerrys." Such satire as this and Mannes' *They* challenge readers to a new image of aging.

# RETIREMENT

While the age for retirement rises and mandatory retirement as a policy is questioned, retirement has remained a major life experience for most men and many women, an experience comparable to birth, marriage, and death in its life-transforming significance. Retirement means working less than full-time year-round at a paying job and deriving income at least in part from Social Security or from a pension. The process of retirement involves separation from the daily work role and usually involves lower income, more leisure time, lessened occupational identification, fewer social contacts with former co-workers, changes in the nature of daily satisfactions, and typically some change of status in the world of work as well as in the community. Changes in the daily schedule lead to changes in family and community relationships for the retiree.

The tasks of assuring adequate income, suitable housing, and appropriate substitute activities (sports, volunteer activity, part-time work, study courses, hobbies, etc.) as well as adjustments of self-concept and attitudes toward aging are of the keenest importance. Identifying or developing new goals for living beyond the worklife is, for most people, an essential task.

Advanced planning in classes, seminars, or on-the-job preparation is now widely available and useful. "Rehearsal" for retirement—looking ahead to anticipate and experiment with new roles, new activities, new sources of support—is a task for those in their forties and fifties. Most of these readings are as much directed to those who are looking ahead as to those whose retirement is at hand. Reading and discussion on this topic come suitably for adults between the ages of 40 and 75.

**The Best Years Book: How to Plan for Fulfillment, Security, and Happiness in the Retirement Years.** Hugh Downs and Richard J. Roll. New York: Delacorte, 1981. 401p. $14.95.

Human and humane, Downs and Roll provide a notably good guide to thinking through retirement years in advance. Practical details are given on diet, health, exercise, family adjustments; financial arrangements both before and after retirement; leisure, learning, and second career possibilities. It has well-organized data, current perspectives and interpretations, and case illustrations in each of these areas. A book worth owning as a manual for important aspects of this phase of life.

For those who find it helpful to view the macro-scene in planning, several titles are worth dipping into from the field of social gerontology. A look at Robert N. Butler's *Why Survive?* (New York: Harper and Row, 1975) for the various sections on retirement would be good. John and C. Davis Hendricks' *Aging in Mass Society* (Englewood Cliffs, N.J.: Winthrop, 1981) discusses flexible retirement, economic conditions of retirement, and devotes a chapter to dilemmas of retirement. Robert C. Atchley's splendid analysis, *The Sociology of Retirement* (Cambridge, Mass.: Schenkman Publishing Co., 1976), is both comprehensive and highly readable.

**Retirement: Creating Promise out of Threat.** Robert K. Kinzel. New York: American Management Association, AMACOM, 1979. 131p. $12.95.

Based on research with men in middle and upper management, this guide to financial planning and to planning use of personal time is clearly directed to middle to upper middle income people. Knowledgeable, balanced, and wise in both the economic and personal decision areas, Kinzel uses his skills as a counselor effectively in the manual. He addresses the text to the reader using a chatty style without losing focus. Attention is given to financial adequacy, social integration, self-respect, satisfying activities, and productive community objectives. Brief, perceptive, this guide might serve well as a basis for retirement discussion groups as well as for individual reading.

The reader of Kinzel's volume may wish to examine W. Robert Walton's *The Retirement Decision: How the New Social Security and Retirement Age Laws Affect You* (New York: Sheed, Andrews, and

McMeel, Inc., 1978) which scrutinizes recent rulings and explains in detail what you might expect to receive from Social Security if retiring at 60, 65, or 70 years of age. Question and answer format. Although this will date quickly with legal changes, the book will remain a good guide to exploring these questions.

**It Takes a Long Time to Become Young.** Garson Kanin. Garden City, N.Y.: Doubleday and Company, 1978. 243p. $10.95; Paper. New York: Berkley Books, 1979. $2.50; Large Type, Boston: G. K. Hall, 1978. $10.95.

A potpourri of anecdotes, sayings, reflections which Kanin weaves into a series of informal essays in praise of anger on forced retirement. This will not only reassure the healthy, competent older adult that life is not over, but functions as well as a sourcebook for those who need cases of famous creative and effective older adults.

More sober and perhaps more objective is *The Graying of Working America: The Coming Crisis in Retirement Age Policy*, by Harold L. Sheppard and Sara E. Rix (New York: Free Press, 1979), which presents a variety of projections of population change and the cost burden of increased numbers of nonworking adults. The authors contend that we must act now to avoid a crisis of support for the nonworking population in future decades.

**The Retirement Handbook.** 6th ed. Joseph C. Buckley. Edited by Henry Schmidt. New York: Harper & Row, 1977. 364p. $9.50; Paper. New York: Barnes & Noble Books, 1977. $4.25.

First published in 1953, Buckley's guide has been the prototype from which all other manuals have grown. Comprehensive and competent in the areas of income planning, housing, retirement employment, this manual now includes detailed attention to retirement to a farm, leisure activities, health and diet, and the importance of the happy acceptance of aging. Subtitled "Complete Guide to Planning Your Future."

**Rehearse before You Retire.** 3d rev. ed. Elmer Otte. Appleton, Wis.: Retirement Research, 1972. 208p. $3.50.

This revised edition has an accompanying *Retirement Rehearsal Guidebook*, 4th ed. (Appleton, Wis.: Retirement Research, 1980. Paper) that is a workbook to accompany the text designed for pre-retirement seminars. Includes inventories, timetables for decision and action, questionnaires to help in decision-making. The text itself provides basic introduction to the major aspects of retirement planning to permit "enjoyment of a well-earned retirement."

**Over 50: The Definitive Guide to Retirement.** Auren Uris. Radnor, Pa.: Chilton Book Company, 1979. 624p. $17.95; Paper. New York: Bantam Books, 1981. $9.95.

Knowledgeable manual and guide to the psychological, social, and economic realities related to retirement and life after work. There is an excellent section on "enriching your life" and equally valid sections on managing time, on health, finances, friends and family, legal rights, and home safety. Valuable services and resources list. Solid middle class orientation.

**The Reality of Retirement: The Inner Experiences of Becoming a Retired Person.** Jules Z. Willing. New York: William Morrow and Company, 1981. 227p. $10.95; Paper $6.95.

Keyed primarily to male business executives' life experience, Willing is sensitive to the particular problems of this life situation. He recognizes, for example, that partial retirement totally deprives the executive of negotiating power. He focuses on planning and decision-making for personal problems related to retirement: whether to move, building new roles in the family, neighborhood, and friendship network. Willing compares life to the two-stage rocket, the first of which provides the drive and thrust to optimum elevation; the second-stage rocket, agile and responsive to new directions, is free of restraint and on a new motive power. Willing sees the second stage launched with retirement and focused on caring involvement in the lives of others, searching for community and new perspectives, allowing life to be a process of becoming. For individual reading or group discussion by business executives.

Richard Bolles' *The Three Boxes of Life: And How to Get Out of Them: An Introduction to Life/Work Planning* (Berkeley, Calif.: Ten Speed Press, 1978) sees retirement as the third life "box": first is education, then comes work, and finally there is leisure. Bolles recommends, as does Willing, that all three aspects of life need development over the full life-span.

**Life Plans: Looking Forward to Retirement.** Grace W. Weinstein. New York: Holt, Rinehart and Winston, 1979. 252p. $9.95; Paper $4.95.

Chatty communication to middle-class Americans in their fifties. Designed to provide a happy, optimistic atmosphere for the prospective retiree. Weinstein focuses on helping the reader to increasing self-knowledge as a basis for making wise choices of when to retire, of what activities to plan, of how to make finances cover needs. These pages of homilies and knowledgeable advice were probably derived from effective lectures.

**Leavetaking: When and How to Say Goodbye.** Mortimer R. Feinberg
and others. New York: Simon & Schuster, 1978. 286p.

Leavetaking is seen as a necessary human process, often involving painful disruption of personal roles. Retirement and job loss is one of these moments. Techniques and strategies for leavetaking are the focus of the book.

RC 12083

**A Time to Enjoy: The Pleasure of Aging.** Lillian R. Dangott and
Richard A. Kalish. Englewood Cliffs, N.J.: Prentice-Hall, 1978.
182p. $11.95; Paper $4.95.

"Our socialization process does not prepare us for living with losses. Learning to do so is one of the major developmental tasks of aging," say Dangott and Kalish. Loss of work status is seen as a major loss. "Retirement must be an adjustment to 'being' as well as to 'doing.' " The authors reinforce the perception of a multi-stage life. See especially pages 116-22.

**Call It Zest: The Vital Ingredient after Seventy.** Elizabeth Yates.
Brattleboro, Vt.: Stephen Greene Press, 1977. 176p.; Large Type.
Boston: G. K. Hall, 1978.

Dynamic profiles of individuals who, although nominally retired, have found that being over 70 need not retire one from active, useful, productive living. Eight men and nine women tell how life can be both rich and meaningful.

**Women, Work, and Volunteering.** Herta Loeser. Boston: Beacon
Press, 1975. 254p.

The co-director of the Civic Center and Clearing House in Boston analyzes the alternatives of paid jobs or volunteer work. She recommends self-analysis based on one's education, experience, training, interests, and needs. Practical advice on writing of resumes and useful listings of resources, services, and bibliographies.

**Threshold: The First Days of Retirement.** Alan H. Olmstead. New
York: Harper & Row, 1975. 214p. $8.95; Large Type. Boston:
G. K. Hall, 1977. $12.50.

Olmstead, a journalist, recounts in brief, manicured two-page journal entries his experience of the first seven months of retirement. He misses the Saturday noon gin rummy crowd; he shares more events with his wife and becomes selective about these; he struggles with each of the tasks suitable to his age: life review, new identity in aging, changes in intergenerational relationships, and so on. He seems to reestablish himself with a new identity coherent with his more familiar self, and acknowledges that as a journalist he found the writing of this journal a help in his adjustment to retirement.

Jean and Robert Hersey's *These Rich Years: A Journal of Retirement* (New York: Charles Scribner & Sons, 1969) is the record from both partners in the retirement of their growth together during the first year. Similarly, Willie Snow Ethridge's *Side by Each* (New York: Vanguard, 1973) recounts the first year in retirement to rural life with her husband. Building the dream house shares the focus with revitalized relationships with family and friends. Good humor and light touches make this especially engaging.

## Creative Literature

**Death of a Salesman.** Arthur Miller. New York: Viking Press, 1949. 139p. $10.00; Paper. New York: Penguin Books, 1976. $2.25.

Willy Loman had been a traveling salesman for his firm since he was 18; he'd started under the original Mr. Wagner. When the new boss, 36-year-old Howard Wagner, forces him to retire rather than give him the in-town job he wants, Willy commits suicide. This provocative play has been a classic statement on forced retirement and has established Willy Loman as the archetypical victim of this problem.

BR 02719; TB 02609; Film. New York: Columbia Broadcasting System, 1966.

**The Price.** Arthur Miller. New York: Viking Press, 1968. 116p.; Paper. New York: Bantam Books, 1969. $1.95.

When Victor Franz must dispose of his father's belongings, his wife Esther calls a dealer listed in an old phone book. Gregory Solomon, a Russian Jew nearly 90 years old, comes to buy the goods. He is very excited to have been called out of retirement and is contrasted to Victor's father, a millionaire who had suffered in the stock market crash and never recovered. A compassionate play that explores the inexorable passage of time.

BR 02218; TB 02244

**You Can't Take It with You.** George Kaufman and Moss Hart. New York: Simon & Schuster, 1937. 207p. In *Three Comedies of American Family Life.* Edited by Joseph E. Mersand. New York: Washington Square Press, 1961. 314p. $3.95.

In this hilarious three-act family play, lifestyle is a central theme. Martin Vanderhof (Grandpa), 75, one day just stopped working 35 years ago. He retired because he didn't want to continue doing work he didn't enjoy. He wanted time "to read, visit the zoo now and then, practice my darts, even have time to notice when spring comes around." He feels that there are always "people that like to work — you can't stop them," but those who don't like it should retire. His daughter Penny and the rest of their relatives are lovable eccentrics. Much of the action revolves around his youngest granddaughter's engagement to the son of a wealthy industrialist. A play that explores values.

BR 00157; CB 00239; Film. Columbia, 1977.

**The Web of Time.** Josephine Lawrence. New York: Harcourt, Brace, Jovanovich, 1953. 304p.

Munsey, 64, is confronted with his imminent mandatory retirement. An old acquaintance, Murtfels, had been forced to retire a few months earlier and commits suicide (pp. 92-106). Although everyone tells Munsey how much he will enjoy his retirement, he doesn't want to leave his work (pp. 52-56), and once retired, he is unable to find another job to help with his family's expenses (pp. 228-48). These sections of the novel are a strong statement against mandatory retirement and its aftermath of personal desolation. The novel is especially weak in its female and its young characters, all of whom are very selfish and unfeeling. Discussable.

**Quartet in Autumn.** Barbara Pym. New York: Harper & Row, 1980. 218p. $2.50; Large Type. Boston: G. K. Hall, 1979. $10.95.

Edwin, Norman, Marcia, and Letty are all about the same age and all work as clerks in the same London office. They are close to retirement; during the novel both women retire and the men begin thinking about their upcoming retirements. After retirement, Letty, a very proper lady, was to move in with her one friend, Marjorie, a widow with a house in the country. But Marjorie becomes engaged and Letty moves to a boardinghouse. Meanwhile, Marcia, who has long been eccentric, dies of malnutrition and other ailments. Norman inherits Marcia's house and realizes not only the security it will give him in retirement but the responsibility that persists among co-workers for one another as human beings.

BR 03903

**Chairman of the Bored.** Edward Streeter. New York: Harper & Row, 1961. 274p.

A humorous, insightful story of a man and his family. The protagonist, Graham Crombie, founder and head of the biggest investment company in America, must retire under a mandatory regulation he initiated years before. Graham and his wife move to a country home in New England but miss New York City so move back a year later. The novel has four sections: Realization, Preparation, Hesitation, and Circuition. Chapter 2 of part 2 (pp. 58-66) is an excellent short piece on Graham's totally unrealistic daydreams of farm life while he contemplates his impending retirement.

BR 08182

**The Second Life of John Stevens.** Paul Eldridge. New York: Thomas Yoseloff, 1960. 204p.

Short reflections and episodes compose this novel about the first year of John Stevens' retirement. As a professor, he had become accustomed to writing and publishing; his wife urges him to review his life through an autobiography. The book concludes with his decision to do so.

**"Brazil."** Paule Marshall. In her *Soul Clap Hands and Sing*, pp. 131-77. Madison, N.J.: Chatham Bookseller, 1971.

The Great Caliban, Brazil's most famous nightclub star, decides to retire from the stage. But he realizes that he doesn't even know Heitor Baptista Guimares, his birth name and identity, any more. Caliban searches for his past through people he used to know, but they all think of him only as Caliban.

# MAINTAINING INCOME

Financial planning for retirement begins with the opening of work life and becomes a matter of money management for a 40-year period or longer. Retirement pension funds, investments (stock, bonds, savings, real estate, etc.), and public funding (Social Security, etc.) become the basis for retirement planning for blue and white collar as well as professional and management workers. After retirement, a shift in location of money resources is typical (from growth funds to income-producing funds) while part-time employment provides a viable supplement for many.

Educated consumer skills stretch the meaning of the dollar, and wise money management (budgeting, wise choice of specialist advisers) extend the significance of retirement income. The selection of readings here focus on general procedures for money management and steps in financial planning. Details on Social Security and retirement funds available in books cited here may soon be outdated, but the problems and the alternatives for solving them will remain useful to the older adult seeking to manage income maintenance.

Income in later years for the poor is dealt with here only in terms of Social Security income. If inflation persists at high rates, and as the percentage of older adults increases within our population, income maintenance will increasingly become a dominant public issue.

**Sylvia Porter's New Money Book for the 80's.** Sylvia Porter. Garden City, N.Y.: Doubleday, 1979. 1305p. $24.95; Paper. New York: Avon Books, 1980. $9.95.

While the entire book is designed for layman's use over a long-term period, the chapter "Planning for Your Financial Security" speaks directly to money management, pensions, housing, and financial traps which those looking ahead to retirement will want to bear in mind.

BR 02873; RC 08564

**Estate Planning for Wives: A Family's Financial Guide.** Merle E. Dowd. Chicago: Regnery, 1971. 260p.

Written for the less knowledgeable person, both men and women will find this a basic and useful guide to money management: investments, insurance, taxes, and similar concerns. Includes guidance on how and where to get needed legal and financial help.

**The Intelligent Woman's Guide to Future Security.** Luis Kutner. New York: Dodd, Mead, 1970. 202p. $4.95.

Designed for women suddenly left in charge of their own affairs. Helpful discussion of wills, probate procedure, estate planning, taxes, insurance, Social Security, real estate, the stock market, financing the funeral. Good introduction to the world of financial records and management.

BR 14336; TB 03268

*Shana Alexander's State-by-State Guide to Women's Legal Rights*, by Shana Alexander with legal consultant help from Barbara Brudno (New York: Wollstonecraft, 1975. BR 15000) will assist widows, divorcees, wives, and single women to understand the legal status they may have in marriage, property, divorce, widowhood, work, rape, crime, and so forth in any of the United States.

**The Star-Spangled Retirement Dream.** James Gollin. New York: Charles Scribner's Sons, 1981. 224p. $12.95.

Detailed explorations of pensions, Social Security, the Employee Retirement Income Security Act (ERISA), the Individual Retirement Account (IRA) with its tax-deferred allowance—all are seen in the context of a financial strategy for retirement. Technical details are clearly set forth for the novice. The book's usefulness is not diminished by recent changes in IRA account allowances.

**Personal Finance.** 6th ed. Jerome B. Cohen. Homewood, Ill.: Richard D. Irwin, 1979. 515p. $18.95.

Textbook style of information on financial planning for life. Comprehensive, detailed, orderly in presentation, this may usefully supplement Gollin on particular matters.

**You and Your Pension.** Ralph Nader and Kate Blackwell. New York: Grossman Publications, 1973. 215p.

Provides the broad background of understanding of current practices in American pension systems and outlines the basic reform measures needed to assure retirees full benefits.

RD 06456

Further clarification and update are available in Bruno Stein's *Social Security and Pensions in Transition* (New York: Free Press, 1980).

**Step-by-Step Guide to Your Retirement Security.** Jack Melnick. New York: New York Times Book Company, 1978. 141p. $8.95.

For the middle-aged adult with children to educate and retirement to plan for, this practical manual outlines the essential steps in financial planning. Obviously some of the data will need updating as time goes, but the procedure is sound and this is a valuable how-to-do-it guide.

Elmer Otte's *Inherit Your Own Money* (New York: David McKay, 1978. BR 10770) presents a practical guide with worksheets and case examples for a responsible, optimistic approach to financing retirement.

**Can You Be Sure of Your Experts? A Complete Manual on How to Choose and Use Doctors, Lawyers, Brokers, and All the Other Experts in Your Life.** Roger A. Golde. New York: Macmillan, 1969. 243p. $5.95.

Important guidance to the layman in choosing advisers in financial, legal, medical, and other special areas of expertise. Covers both selection (how to check out an expert's qualification) and collaboration (the distinct roles for the expert and for the client).

Hugh Downs and Richard J. Roll's *The Best Years Book* (New York: Delacorte, 1981) and Leonard Biegel's *The Best Years Catalogue* (New York: Putnam's Sons, 1978) are highly useful (as are the other general guides to retirement information) in providing leads to expert advice, whether from organizations or agencies specializing in the particular problem the older adult may face.

**Consumer Survival Kit.** John Dorfman. New York: Praeger, 1975. 302p. $3.95.

Consumer skills that stretch the dollar for its greatest value are part of maintaining income in retirement years. Dorfman's adaptation of the television series from the Maryland Center for Public Broadcasting provides guidance in supermarket strategy, old and new housing, tenants rights, air fare bargains, cost effectiveness in funerals and service stations, and a multitude of money concerns for people with limited income. Compact, practical, sensible.

BR 03336

Amram M. Ducovny's *The Billion Dollar Swindle: Frauds against the Elderly* (New York: Fleet Press Corp., 1969. TB 03291) exposes schemes to "help" the elderly and shows the reader how to spot them.

**Marketing Your Skills after Retirement.** Juvenal L. Angel. New York: World Trade Press, Inc., 1975. 86p.

Specific, practical advice on getting a new job as a retired person, on creating your own job in the home, starting your own business, or locating the right kind of part-time work. The perspective is as much on enjoyable use of leisure time as on supplementary income.

Lillian E. Troll, with Joan and Kenneth Israel, has edited *Looking Ahead: A Woman's Guide to the Problems and Joys of Growing Older* (Englewood Cliffs, N.J.: Prentice-Hall, 1977), which includes a chapter on older women and jobs.

**Radical Career Change: Life beyond Work.** David L. Krantz. New York: Free Press, 1978. 157p. $9.95.

For those who retired with joy in freedom and yet find a work life an enjoyable lifestyle, Krantz's interviews with some thirty Santa Fe residents who made the mid-life career switch (some of them at retirement) may prove interesting. No specific guidance on such career changes is to be found here, but reflection on the meaningfulness of the work life and the potential in radical lifestyle change may be welcome.

## Creative Literature

**Diary of an Old Man.** Chaim Bermant. New York: Holt, Rinehart and Winston, 1967. 191p.

Through the diary of 84-year-old Cyril we experience living on a severely reduced income. He chooses between heat and food, walks to save busfare, and spends his days at the park and the library. During the month that the diary is kept, Cyril suffers two serious losses — his safe, inexpensive apartment when his landlady dies, and his only surviving friend, George. A stark and moving portrayal.

**"John Barton Rosedale, Actor's Actor."** John O'Hara. In his *The Hat on the Bed*, pp. 129-43. New York: Random House, 1962.

"Rosey," age 67, lost a lot of money in the stock market, so he and his wife Millicent live on a very tight budget. When he refuses a small acting role because he is accustomed to playing the lead, Millicent feels he has made a mistake ... again! Poignant human dilemma.

# WHERE TO LIVE

The "young old" and the "old old" may have quite different answers to the question of where to live. The maintenance of independent living for independent people is a high priority, but as physical or psychological dependence comes with advancing years, a change in living arrangements is often necessary.

For the affluent and healthy retiree, the choice of places to live is rich: at home? overseas? in a retirement village? The Dickinson guides to geographic location are excellent. For moves to a new home, the Herseys and the Nearings have delightful experiences and wisdom to share. Irwin has superb counsel on selling your present home, while Longbotham and Smith suggest ways to make your present home more livable. Cooley, Vining, and Curtin each provide perspective on retirement communities for the affluent. Low-income housing opportunities are increasingly available, and such guides as Downs and Roll's *Best Years Book* direct users to proper sources of information on these.

When we must make decisions with older parents or relatives (or for ourselves) on their (or our) relinquishment of independent living, the choices are more difficult. Poe discusses adapting your home to accommodate an older person. Burger and D'Erasmo, as well as Nassau and Galton, provide an understanding of how to choose a nursing home. The "culture shock" of entering a nursing home is made understandable by May Sarton, by Laird, and by several other writers. Housing the "old old," the ill, the disoriented, the poor, is still a major social problem of our times; the human import of the problem is best understood in the short stories, novels, and plays that probe this human experience.

**Sunbelt Retirement: The Complete State-by-State Guide to Retiring in the South and West of the United States.** Peter A. Dickinson. New York: E. P. Dutton, 1980. 338p. $14.95; Paper $8.50 each; Large Type. Boston: G. K. Hall, n.d. 2 vols.

Climate, living costs, leisure and cultural facilities, health care, housing alternatives, special services for seniors, economic well-being of the area, tax policies—all may influence the choice of location in retirement, whether to move and where. Dickinson presents summary evaluations state by state. Updating of the data may be done through easily accessible information sources in the average public library.

*Retirement Edens Outside the Sunbelt* by Peter A. Dickinson (New York: E. P. Dutton, 1981) provides similar coverage of analysis for the states outside the Sunbelt. Dickinson provides the interesting statistic that only 15% of retirees move any distance from their pre-retirement residences.

**Where to Retire on a Small Income: Where to Enjoy the Good Life on Little.** Norman D. Ford. Floral Park, N.Y.: Harian Books, n.d. 274p. Pamphlet $4.95.

First published in 1950 and frequently revised. Low living costs and pleasant surroundings are the criteria for inclusion of cities, towns, and farms throughout the continental United States, Hawaii, Puerto Rico, and the Virgin Islands. Includes information on retirement hotels as well.

**Change in the Wind.** Jean and Robert Hersey. New York: Charles Scribner's Sons, 1972. 248p.

Jean and Robert Hersey write a delightful, unselfconscious account of their life experience in relocation of their home from Weston, Connecticut, to North Carolina. A compatible couple with many interests and hobbies which their comfortable wealth allows them to indulge, the Herseys revel in nature, gardens, in their many friends. This will be a welcome analysis of the decision on relocation for readers who share the background and interests of the Herseys. Some readers may be turned off by concerns for the "black brethren," while others may be offended by the emotional trauma induced by the sacrifice of the Connecticut orchid greenhouse. But this is a delightful personal biography of a year of decision.

TB 04802

**The Old Person in Your Home.** William D. Poe. New York: Charles Scribner's Sons, 1969. 180p.

A family doctor with understanding of the psychological as well as the physical needs of the elderly writes of the necessity of making the older person feel loved and wanted, and offers sensible advice not only on medical problems and resources but also on living arrangements in the home and various day-to-day situations.

**Living in a Nursing Home: A Complete Guide for Residents, Their Families and Friends.** Sarah Green Burger and Martha D'Erasmo. New York: Continuum Publishing, 1976. 178p. $8.95.

Written by two nurses with a number of years of experience working with the elderly in nursing homes, this is a guide to preparing for and selecting a nursing home, the process of admission, and assuring that the transition avoids trauma but sustains family and community relationships. This is designed for the elderly as well as their families.

Numerous guides on selecting nursing homes provide criteria for evaluating them. Jean Baron Nassau's *Choosing a Nursing Home* is a typical good one (New York: Funk and Wagnall's Publishing Co., 1975). Lawrence Galton offers a full chapter on nursing homes and their alternatives in his *Don't Give Up on an Aging Parent* (New York:

Crown Publishers, 1975), while Sharon R. Curtin provides a chapter on retirement communities and life care centers (their pros and cons) as well as good advice on convalescent hospitals and nursing home care (pp. 141-59) in her *Nobody Ever Died of Old Age* (Boston: Little, Brown, 1972).

**Tender Loving Greed: How the Incredibly Lucrative Nursing Home "Industry" Is Exploiting America's Old People and Defrauding Us All.** Mary Adelaide Mendelson. New York: Random House, 1975. 245p. $2.95.

Such exposures as this in the best muckraking tradition in the middle 1970s have brought about much needed regulation and reform, but the problems identified here still remain inherent in the nursing home situation. This is a volume for all who assist in determining the selection of a nursing home, since many excellent nursing homes now exist and can demonstrate their competence under informed questioning of those who apply for admission.

RD 07250

Linda Horn and Elma Griesel's *Nursing Homes: A Citizens' Action Guide* (Boston: Beacon Press, 1977. RC 16199) provides a strategy for change and reform in laws and legislation, inspection, and in enforcement of residents' rights.

**Living the Good Life: How to Live Sanely and Simply in a Troubled World.** Helen and Scott Nearing. New York: Schocken Books, 1970. 213p. $9.95; Paper $4.95.

The poet Scott Nearing and his wife Helen describe their life on a Vermont farm where they have subsisted for 20 years as a satisfying alternative lifestyle. They specifically recommend this to active people searching for an environment in which to spend their later years.

**The $100,000 Decision: The Older American's Guide to Selling a Home and Choosing Retirement Housing.** Robert Irwin. New York: McGraw-Hill Book Company, 1981. 188p. $14.95.

A seasoned real estate broker and skilled writer on his specialty, Irwin provides clear interpretation of the tax-free capital gains option open to those over 55 years of age who sell their home. Alternative housing is explored with similar knowledgeability on costs and the bases for housing choices. Detailed authoritative guidance.

**Make Your Home Comfortable for Retirement.** Marion Longbotham. Madison: Wisconsin Cooperative Extension Programs,
n.d. B2165.

Suggestions for making home safer, more comfortable,
convenient, and satisfying. A second Longbotham pamphlet, *Select
Your Retirement Housing* (Madison: Wisconsin Cooperative
Extension Programs, n.d. B2164) identifies the factors to consider in
making housing choices.

**The Pursuit of Dignity: New Living Alternatives for the Elderly.** Bert
Kruger Smith. Boston: Beacon Press, 1977. 154p. $9.95; Paper
$4.45; Large Type. Boston: G. K. Hall, 1978. $11.50.

The author explores the alternatives that give the housing,
nutrition, and psychological uplift that the elderly need.
BRA 16039

**How to Avoid the Retirement Trap.** Leland Frederick Cooley and
Lee Morrison Cooley. New York: Nash Publishing Corporation,
1972. 285p.

Among diverse topics addressed (investments, travel's advantages
and disadvantages), the Cooleys discuss living as older persons in
Mexico and the pros and cons of housing complexes of different kinds
designed for older persons.

**Being Seventy: The Measures of a Year.** Elizabeth Gray Vining.
New York: Viking Press, 1978. 194p. $10.00; Large Type.
Boston: G. K. Hall, 1978. 289p. $11.50.

This journal of her seventieth year takes Elizabeth Gray Vining
back to Japan to visit the Emperor to whom she had served as a tutor,
forward to Harvard for an honorary degree, deep into contemplation
of aging, and into a new experiment in living in a retirement
community. A rich, fulfilling year indeed!
RD 13697

**Home Life: A Story of Old Age.** Dorothy Rabinowitz and Yedida
Nielson. New York: Macmillan, 1971. 192p.

The battle for a lifestyle of dignity and independence in nursing
homes is depicted in this readable and poignant presentation of daily
life and activities under institutional auspices. Condescension rather
than caring, decisions made for rather than with the resident, daily
choices reduced to a minimum—perhaps inevitable numerous acts

that add up to emasculation of vital individuality. Important reading for families and friends so that they may know what compensating styles are needed from them as they visit and interact with their loved older persons.

Corabeth Laird, an 84-year-old established author and anthropologist, recounts her experience of a 10-week stay in a nursing home before rescue by a family of close friends who opened their home to her. *Limbo* (Novato, Calif.: Chandler and Sharp, 1979. RD 14925) details the problems of poor food, incompetent aides, daily mingling of the mentally incompetent with the competent elderly. She gradually succumbed, in weakness and ill health, to the dehumanizing effect of being treated as senile—until it became known that she was about to have a book published. The revealing transformation in behavior toward her documents the human situation for those who perhaps do not write books!

**Dying in the Sun.** Donn Pearce. New York: Charterhouse Books, 1974. 248p.

A vivid, angry report on the miseries of old people in Florida who remain in independent living with physical disabilities, inadequate income, and loss of contact with families. Miami and other parts of south Florida have such numbers of the elderly in this situation that social services (Rescue Squads, etc.) find much of their attention directed to what has become a major social problem as well as individual tragedy.

RD 07511

## *Creative Literature*

**Sadie Shapiro's Knitting Book.** Robert K. Smith. New York: Simon & Schuster, 1973. 190p.; Large Type. Boston: G. K. Hall, 1973.

Sadie Shapiro's vibrant personality and love of life surmount and then transform the "old folks" home to which she retired. When fame and fortune come to her with the publication of her book, she chooses not to leave her contacts with friends in the home but to marry one of her friends there and to remain "Sadie." Witty, often hilarious episodes that have a terribly authentic ring.

BRA 15385; RD 07139

**Years Are So Long.** Josephine Lawrence. New York: Frederick A. Stokes Co., 1934. 309p.

Barkley and Lucy Cooper are rotated among their five children's homes when they are no longer able to afford to keep their own home. Although they protest, the children separate them so that none of them have both parents at one time. When Barkley dies at the end of the novel, Lucy is sent to a nursing home against her wishes. Excellently written, this novel is depressing in its portrayal of the lack of understanding of the middle-aged toward their elders.

Film. *Make Way for Tomorrow*. Paramount, 1937.

Lawrence wrote a second book on the theme of middle-aged children sharing responsibility for their parents. *All Our Tomorrows* (New York: Harcourt, 1959) explores the problems which arise when four generations share a household. The first chapter (pp. 1-31) is representative of the book and would be a good discussion-starter.

**"The Old Woman and Her Cat."** Doris Lessing. In *Solo: Women on Women Alone*, pp. 332-48. Edited by Linda Hamalian and Leo Hamalian. New York: Dell, 1977. 367p. $1.95.

Hetty is a shopping bag lady who dies of exposure in an abandoned building. She has moved there to avoid institutionalization when she is evicted from her apartment building for having a cat. A moving and evocative story. "Management" by Margaret Lamb (pp. 25-40) tells the tale of Bitsy Larkin, who is faced with a similar problem. In order to avoid the terror of a nursing home, she lives in an unsafe building and neighborhood, and retains her independence in an untraditional fashion.

**The Stone Angel.** Margaret Laurence. New York: Bantam, 1981. 304p. $2.95; Large Type. London, Ont.: Gatefold Ltd., 1964.

Marvin Shipley and his wife, both in their mid-sixties, feel that they are no longer able to care for his sick mother, Hagar, who is 90. They take her on "a ride in the country" which is really a trip to see Silver Threads, the nursing home they have chosen for her (pp. 81-94). To avoid being sent there, Hagar runs away and hides out in an abandoned cannery. At the end of the novel her powerlessness over her fate is clear as she is found ill and returned to the home for her final days.

BRA 03038

Another piece, dealing with an elder's decision to avoid a nursing home his children have selected, deserves note. *Fadeout* by Douglas Woolf (New York: Grove, 1959) recounts the experience of Dick Twombly, a retired banker of 74, who tires of being treated like a baby by his daughter and her family. When they decide to put him in a nursing home, he hitchhikes to Arizona and starts a new life. The first chapter (pp. 1-45) is an especially good portrayal of the indignities he suffers in his daughter's household.

**"The Flood."** Patricia Zelver. In her *A Man of Middle Age and Twelve Other Stories*, pp. 203-218. New York: Holt, Rinehart and Winston, 1980. 278p. $12.95.

A fiercely independent, eccentric, 75-year-old widow, Hilda Butterwick, lives alone in her primitive old hunting lodge, "The Chalet." Her daughters feel that she should move to The Manse, a modern nursing home, but Hilda refuses. During a bad storm, John Brigham, an elderly lawyer who once was Hilda's beau but is no longer on speaking terms with her, arranges for someone to rescue Hilda. She refuses, however, and dies in the flood while riding the roof of her home. John knows that she has "triumphed over him irrevocably" because he'll end up in a nursing home eventually.

**I Was Dancing.** Edwin O'Connor. Boston: Little, Brown, 1964. 242p.

Tom and Ellen Considine arrange for his father Daniel, a retired vaudeville dancer, to move into Smiling Valley, an old people's home, where his sister Delia lives. But Daniel prefers to remain in their home and plots to stay there until Tom finally has a therapeutic and clarifying showdown. The rights of adult children to live their own lives are put into balance with the desires of the older parent.

TB 00541

**Marty.** Paddy Chayefsky. In his *Television Plays*, pp. 133-72. New York: Simon & Schuster, 1955. 268p.; Paper 1971. $5.95.

A similar theme is explored in the strong subplot of this moving play. Theresa lives with her 36-year-old unmarried son, Marty. Her sister, Catherine, has been living with her son and daughter-in-law, but moves in with Theresa when the other arrangement becomes impossible. The two sisters discuss the problems of living with their grown children. The film stresses this subplot more than the play does.

Film. United Artists, 1955.

**I Never Sang for My Father.** Robert Anderson. New York: Random House, 1968. 115p.

Deals with the relationship of middle-aged children and older parents who need a place to live. After the death of his wife, Tom

Garrison is alone in his house. His 40-year-old son, Gene, is engaged to be married and is planning to move away. Alice, Gene's sister, feels strongly that Gene should pursue his plans and find a housekeeper for their father. Gene also looks at nursing homes but does not want to institutionalize his father. Although this moving play is written from the perspective of the middle-aged son, Gene, it is a good portrayal of the housing problems of an ill older person.

Film. Columbia, 1969; film clip, Act 2, "When Parents Grow Old [Housing]," Learning Corporation of America, 1972.

**As We Are Now.** May Sarton. New York: Norton, 1973. 136p. $10.95.

After Caro Spencer at 76 has a heart attack, her house is closed and she moves in with her brother and his wife. When this arrangement doesn't work out for anyone, including Caro, she is sent to Twin Pines, a small rural nursing home. It is a typical institution in which the lack of independence, the insensitivities of the staff, and the social isolation become unbearable for her. Written as her journal, the novel ends with an afterword making clear her final horrible rebellion.

RD 07015

**Apostles of Light.** Ellen Douglas. Boston: Houghton Mifflin, 1973. 307p.

Martha Clarke at 77 is living alone in the old family home in Homochitt, Mississippi now that her sister has died. The family has a conference on what to do about the situation (pp. 1-29) and decides to let her remain there if a distant relative, Howie Snyder, boards there and helps out. He turns the house into Golden Age, a nursing home with inept and abusive employees. The old people there become victims. This is another sensitizing novel.

RD 07313

**"Old Man Minnick."** Edna Ferber. In *Intimate Relationships: Marriage, Family, and Lifestyles through Literature*, pp. 225-39. Englewood Cliffs, N.J.: Prentice-Hall, 1975. 480p. $16.95; Paper $11.95.

In this story, a retirement home is viewed positively, as a pleasant alternative to living with children and grandchildren. After Ma's unexpected death, Pa moves in with his son, George, and George's wife, Nettie. He misses being spoiled and loved by his wife. He also misses being listened to and valued. Once he discovers that the nearby park is full of old men, he goes there every day. One main topic of conversation is life with the kids vs. life in the Grant Home for Aged Gentlemen. Ferber's opinion is that those who live with their children are proud to be wanted, but tend to be poorly groomed and always busy with domestic talk, chores, and errands. The residents of the home, however, are proud of their independence, impeccably groomed, and devoted to intelligent conversation. At the end of the story, Old Man Minnick happily moves into the Grant Home to be with his new friends.

**All the Years of Her Life.** Josephine Lawrence. New York: Harcourt, Brace, Jovanovich, 1972. 182p.

Three middle-aged friends, Edie Cummings, Stacy Allen, and Clover Mills, share the problem of having elderly parents for whom they are responsible. Edie's and Stacy's daughters solve everyone's dilemma by finding an apartment for all of the older people to live in with the middle-aged children (fourteen in all) paying the rent. This scheme works so well that the novel ends with their considering buying a whole apartment building for seniors to live in. The last two chapters (pp. 146-82) can stand independently for discussion. A caution: The novel assumes that only the daughters, and not the sons, are concerned about their parents. Nevertheless, the last two parts of the novel are good discussion-starters.

**Retreat with Honor.** Josephine Lawrence. New York: Harcourt, Brace, Jovanovich, 1973. 220p. $6.95; Large Type, Boston: G. K. Hall, 1973. 359p.

This novel explores the subject of senior communal living in a model retirement community for people over 60. Homesite, a millionaire philanthropist's project, is wildly popular and spawns a second, called Peace Haven. In both, most of the problems concern the young: irate middle-aged children who want to leave their kids with the grandparents; teenagers who want to bicycle or dance during their visits; holiday conflicts, etc. As in many of her novels, all young people are stereotyped as stupid or selfish. Yet good issues and ideas are presented. Section 2 of chapter 2 (pp. 18-33) is representative of the whole and focuses on Corey's fiftieth anniversary party as the main event.

RD 06907

**Tell Me a Riddle.** Tillie Olsen. New York: Delacorte, 1978. $8.95; New York: Dell Publications, 1976. $2.25.

After 47 years of marriage and five children, Pa feels that he and Ma should move to the Haven, a retirement community run by his lodge. She doesn't want to leave her house and home. Part 1 of this four-part novella is especially evocative on this theme. In part 3, after she is diagnosed as having cancer, and he has secretly sold their house, they move to a retirement community in Florida.

Film. Godmother Productions, 1980.

**The Mother.** Paddy Chayefsky. In his *Television Plays*, pp. 181-218. New York: Simon & Schuster, 1955. 268p.; 1971. $5.95.

To the mother, keeping her own apartment and retaining her independence are one and the same. But her daughter Annie can't understand why her 66-year-old mother insists on looking for work to earn enough money to keep her apartment. Although George, Annie's husband, is agreeable to the idea of the mother living with them, he is able to understand her point of view and to convince Annie to respect her mother's needs.

**"Old Man Warner."** Dorothy Canfield Fisher. In her *A Harvest of Stories from Half a Century of Writing*, pp. 23-28. New York: Harcourt, Brace, Jovanovich, 1956. 352p.

Old Man Warner, a 71-year-old widower, decides to stay on his farm alone rather than move in with his sons who live in another state. He has lived there for 22 years and even his neighbors can't convince him to leave. "We found we were proud of him, as proud as could be, the darned old bulldog, who had stuck it out all alone in spite of us."

TB 01885

# FAMILY LIFE AND
# FAMILY RELATIONSHIPS

Our stereotypic perceptions of aging (in ourselves and in other members of our family) create serious destruction in personal relationships within the family. We make assumptions about aging that force changes in the relationship between husband and wife (whether in sexual activity or in household responsibilities), in closeness to sons and daughters (who may unconsciously be displacing the parent in power roles or who may be victimized by the parent's desperate hold on power), in sharing in the nurture of grandchildren (who are, after all, the children of their parents). As society forces the older person to new self-perceptions, the strains of adjustment may be projected on the marriage partner or on the adult daughter or son. Hostility or suspicion may come to divide the family. Mental health, sound self-respect and respect for others, on the other hand, may permit open communication and resolution to the problems inevitable in the adjustment to change. Sturdy independence or a rebellious spirit are part of a struggle for survival of the individual. Self-understanding, self-acceptance, and acceptance by others are vital to equanimity and peace within the family circle.

The door to understanding the family adjustments in aging is only beginning to open. Some of the more complex and significant relationships are better portrayed and understood in creative literature and become manageable as one explores such fictional (but how true!) dilemmas with others in group discussion.

**Families in Later Life.** Lillian E. Troll, Sheila J. Miller, and Robert C. Atchley. Belmont, Calif.: Wadsworth Publishers, 1979. 168p.

A formal exploration of family lives of older people, including those who have never married or never become parents.

**Retirement: Coping with Emotional Upheavals.** Leland P. and Mary I. Bradford. Chicago: Nelson-Hall, 1979. 202p. $8.95.

The marriage relationship is put under stress with retirement of either spouse. Leland and Martha Bradford, experienced in human communication and in open relationship training, here reveal their own adjustment problems and then discuss the range of situations and solutions that are open to married couples in their fifties and sixties. While good reading on its own, this book will prove an excellent source for group reading and discussion among couples in study group style.

Jean and Robert Hersey's *These Rich Years* (New York: Charles Scribner and Sons, 1969) and Alan Olmstead's *Threshold: The First Days of Retirement* (New York: Harper & Row, 1975; Large Type. Boston: G. K. Hall, 1977) provide highly personal illustrations of many of the situations about which the Bradfords talk.

**This Timeless Moment.** Laura Archera Huxley. Millbrae, Calif.: Celestial Arts, 1968. 330p.; Paper 1975. $4.95.

Laura and Aldous Huxley are drawn deeply together as his wife enters Huxley's spiritual world during the days he is approaching death.

**The Fires of Autumn: Sexual Activity in the Middle and Later Years.** Peter Q. Dickinson. New York: Drake Publishers, Inc., 1974. 192p.; Paper, New York: Sterling Publisher, 1977. $4.95.

Accepting sexual drives as fundamental to human well-being throughout life, Dickinson provides a useful illumination of how these were dealt with in other times and cultures before he details our current orientation to sex and to sex in the older years. He discusses the life phases' influence on sex through the female menopause and examines the relationship of heart attacks, strokes, prostate surgery, and various other illnesses to the exercise of sexual needs. This volume was one of the early frank explorations that helped to explode the myth that adults are sexless after sixty-five. The enrichment of companionship in married relationships in the later years by sexual activity is the focal concern of this authoritative volume.

# GRANDPARENTING

**A Book for Grandmothers.** Ruth Goode. New York: Macmillan, 1976. 228p.; Paper, New York: McGraw-Hill Book Co., 1977. $3.95.

Sensible, practical advice as useful to grandfathers as to grandmothers. Advice on all types of situations in intergenerational living, from grandparent interventions to the giving of money and gifts (when and how). Background information for grandparents on divorce (when their adult children face this), sexual freedom expected by the very young generation, and similar cluing in the older generation to values and assumptions in the grandchildren's environment. Excellent guidebook to the new experience for older adults.

RD 10249

Even more step-by-step advice for the novice in Lanie Carter's *Congratulations! You're Going to Be a Grandmother* (San Diego, Calif.: Oak Tree Publications, 1980), which advocates a loving, nonjudgmental approach.

**How to Grandparent.** Fitzhugh Dodson with Paula Reuben. New York: Harper & Row, Publishers, 1981. 304p. $10.95.

The role of grandparent as nurturer can be played well only if the grandparent is knowledgeable in child development, appropriate play activities, and intellectual growth at each stage, so the authors provide this up-to-date background. The role of grandparents at long-distance and in single-parent families is discussed. Lists of recommended toys and equipment, books and records for each developing stage to give emotional support and intellectual stimulation are provided.

## Creative Literature

**"The Sudden Sixties."** Edna Ferber. In her *One Basket: 31 Short Stories*, pp. 198-214. New York: Doubleday, 1957. 581p. $3.95.

An eloquent story of a widow caught in the role of perpetual babysitter for her grandchildren. Hannah Winter, 60, is startled to see herself as haggard and old. Widowed for 23 years, she had worked hard to raise her children alone, and now she cherishes her leisure time. But her daughter Marcia lives nearby and needs her to babysit. Althugh Hannah resents it she cannot seem to refuse to help.

**"Old Mrs. Harris."** Willa Cather. In her *Obscure Destinies*. New York: Random House, 1974. 229p. $1.95.

Grandma Harris lives with her daughter Victoria and her family where she works as a servant in the household. A neighbor, Mrs. Rosen, feels that Mrs. Harris is mistreated and should be respected and catered to the way her family had always behaved. But Mrs. Harris doesn't want to trouble anyone. She waits to die until she knows that her eldest granddaughter will be able to go to college; then she dies quietly and quickly.

BR 09986

**"Lullabies."** Joanne Greenberg. In her *Summering: A Book of Short Stories*, pp. 69-80. New York: Holt, Rinehart and Winston, 1966. 208p. $4.95.

From infancy through high school, Jane has spent every Sunday with her Grandpa with whom she had a special relationship. But when she and her boyfriend Rudy decide to move to the slums to do social welfare work, Grandpa can no longer accept or understand his Jane.

**"The Leader of the People."** John Steinbeck. In *The Red Pony*, pp. 73-92. New York: Bantam Books, 1975; Large Type. New York: National Association for the Visually Handicapped, n.d.

Jody, a young boy, adores his grandfather and his stories about leading the people across the plains. Jody's parents, however, are tired of the stories and impatient with Grandfather. Although mother respects him out of duty, father is rude to him. Only Jody understands how wounding the adults can be to a person's pride. A simple and lovely story about the bonds between a grandfather and grandson.

    BR 00612; CB 00324; Film. Phoenix Films, 1974.

**A Killing Frost.** Sylvia Wilkinson. Boston: Houghton Mifflin, 1967. 216p.

    Thirteen-year-old Ramona is home from school for Christmas vacation when her grandmother, with whom she lives, has a stroke. The last two chapters (pp. 204-216) are especially descriptive of Ramie's reaction to her grandmother's disability and of the reactions of the other family members who are condescending to their elderly eccentric relative.

# AGING PARENTS

**Growing Old Is a Family Affair.** Dorothy Bertolet Fritz. Atlanta, Ga.: John Knox Press, 1972. unp. $2.95.

    Written for the family unit, this book touches lightly yet seriously on awareness of aging and death, both for the young-old and for the old-old as well as for the middle-aged and younger adults. Joyousness and the privilege of life are emphasized while adjusting to or circumventing the problems of aging.

**Getting along with Your Grown-up Children.** Helen S. Arnstein. New York: M. Evans and Company, 1970. 208p. $5.95.

    Directed to the older parent, this wise book of guidance to the new set of problems in the parent-child relationship points out changes in both child and parent and how their relationship is affected by this fact. Discusses questions of role in family, independence, control, marriage. The decade since its publication has not vastly altered the soundness of this advice.

    Tx-BPH (CBT 2836) RC

**The Other Generation Gap: The Middle-Aged and Their Aging Parents.** Stephen Z. Cohen and Bruce M. Gans. Chicago: Follett, 1978. 290p. $10.95; Paper. "Other Generation Gap: You and Your Aging Parents. New York: Warner Books, 1980. $2.95.

Addressed directly to the adult son or daughter of an aging parent, this book facilitates an understanding of health and role losses of the older person and the difficult, intertwined reactions of parent and adult child in a reversal of dependency roles under these circumstances. "Practically every parent-child relationship is made up of powerful, dimly understood feelings of love, hate, grief, guilt, resentment and compassion ... often living side by side in an uneasy equilibrium" (p. 227). A summary chapter of principles provides a "healthy frame of reference" for adult child/aging parent relationships. The body of the book, however, provides the needed experience for the middle-aged adult in feeling the older adult's dilemmas and needs.

Edgar Jackson's *Coping with the Crisis in Your Life* (New York: Hawthorne Books, 1974; Paper. New York: Aronson, Jason, Inc., 1980) examines the crises that occur in the various stages of adult life, including the changing relationships of parents and adult children.

**Summer of the Great Grandmother.** Madeleine L'Engle. New York: Farrar, Straus, & Giroux, 1974. 245p. $10.95; Paper. New York: Seabury Press, 1980. $5.95.

L'Engle writes of her own family—her dying mother, her maturing son, her small grandchild—in the four-generation summer home in New England. While she works through her support to her mother, her guilt and compassion, she also finds she must shift her role with her son who now is able to exert leadership in meeting family crises. Warm, human record of facing death in the several generations, and a wonderful demonstration that the complex mesh of family life is the context within which major crises and events are played out.

RC 09165

**Aging Is a Family Affair.** Victoria E. Bumagin and Kathryn F. Hirn. New York: Harper & Row/Crowell, 1979. 276p. $10.95.

An anecdotal orientation of the young or middle-aged adult to the realities of aging in the 1980s in our society, this guidebook for the elderly and their families is warm and understanding. Focus is on the independent older adult, the continuity of his or her life interests and activities, financial dilemmas and solutions, psychological needs and their satisfactions. The chapters on death, dying, and grief are direct, sympathetic, and wise.

RC 15697

**You and Your Aging Parent.** Barbara Silverstone and Helen Kandel Hyman. New York: Pantheon Books, 1982. 320p. $15.95; Paper $8.95.

A fully rounded perspective on the family context within which the parent ages, this analysis is addressed to the middle-aged offspring, but will equally well meet needs of parents in their fifties or sixties who are prepared to become self-aware. The authors, with husbands whose help in psychiatry and sociology is acknowledged, have sensitively explored a multitude of problem areas and concerns in an open, constructive fashion. Switch in roles, guilt and anger, "caretaker" problems; the games old people play; the human dilemmas of the older parent; the family and community solutions; legislative and public action—all are given skillful attention for the person trapped in this common dilemma of love and the need for freedom.

Mi-BPH (MSL-3931) RM

A briefer manual, drawing on the Silverstone and Hyman as well as other useful guides, Margaret J. Anderson's *Your Aging Parents: When and How to Help* (St. Louis: Concordia Publishing House, 1979) focuses on how to view the increasing dependence of an independent parent. Approaches to housing, finances, health, drugs, institutional care, and death are explored with sane and human concern for sustaining the loving relationship in the context of help. Anderson includes a bibliography and directory of where to go for help.

**Caring for Your Aged Parents.** Earl A. Grollman and Sharon Hya Grollman. Boston: Beacon Press and Harper, 1978. 160p. $4.95.

As professional counselors, the Grollmans (father and daughter) have created for sons and daughters of aging parents an experiential introduction to an empathetic understanding of aging. This lays the foundation for a new compassionate relationship that can apply as well among all family (or even neighborhood) relationships.

**Strategies for the Second Half of Life.** Peter Weaver. New York: Franklin Watts, 1980. 394p. $12.95.

While covering many basic concerns, the situation of the aging person responsible for aging parents is uniquely addressed here.

**Don't Give Up on an Aging Parent.** Lawrence Galton. New York: Crown Publishers, 1974. 240p. $6.95.

As a doctor specializing in geriatric medicine, Galton looks at the elderly as human beings with medical and other human problems that deserve attention and solution. He is concerned that the elderly are often "written off" as senile when careful analysis would identify a problem which some small adjustment could eliminate.

**Fighting Angel: Portrait of a Soul.** Pearl S. Buck. New York: Reynal & Hitchcock, 1936. 302p.

This autobiographical account describes the author's attempts to make her father's last few years happy and comfortable despite differences in temperament and viewpoint.

RC 12846; TB 00543

**Gramp.** Mark Jury and Dan Jury. New York: Grossman, 1976. 152p.; Paper. New York: Penguin Books, 1978. $6.95.

Richly human but unsentimental record in pictures and words of the last days of Gramp, the senile grandfather whom a family decided to care for at home. The problems, the patience, the caring, the grief, the ritual of death — all are here with three generations sharing the family event.

**Mazel Tov! You're Middle-aged.** Albert Vorspan. Garden City, N.Y.: Doubleday, 1974. 128p.

Uproarious guide to dealing with middle age and beyond. In a humorous manner, the author discusses the changing role of parents with their children. Encourages becoming a person rather than dwelling on wondering if the kids will eat right.

RD 07161

**Survival Handbook for Children of Aging Parents.** Arthur N. Schwartz. Chicago: Follett, 1977. 160p. $6.95.

A book to help middle-aged children develop an honest dialogue with their older parents in the hope that they can approach their aging parents openly for true communication.

## Creative Literature

**Dad.** William Wharton. New York: Knopf, 1981. 416p. $12.95; Paper. New York: Avon Books, 1981. $3.50.

In this extremely powerful novel about father-son relationships, the first person perspective changes among John Tremond, 52, John's father, Jack, 71, and John's son, Billy, teen-aged. When John is called back to California because his mother is ill, he must cope with his Dad as well as his son. At the end of the novel, John is once more headed for California. This time he is going to his father's funeral, with a new understanding of what his father's life had been about.

**I Never Sang for My Father.** Robert Anderson. New York: Random House, 1968. 115p.

An evocative portrayal of the father-son relationship. Tom Garrison, nearly 80, is a difficult, argumentative man who has been estranged from his daughter, Alice, for many years and has a difficult relationship with his son, Gene. At the end of the first act, Tom's wife Margaret dies; both Tom and Gene mourn her loss, and try to become closer. At Tom's death, Gene says, "Death ends a life ... but it does not end a relationship, which struggles in the survivor's mind toward some resolution."

Film. Columbia, 1970.

Another especially good piece on the father-son relationship is the first chapter of Wallace Stegner's *Angle of Repose* (New York: Doubleday, 1971; New York: Fawcett Book Group, 1978). Rodman Ward is trying to get his father, Lyman, to assume a less independent lifestyle now that he is wheelchair-bound. But Lyman, 58, wants to continue living in his grandmother's cottage, writing his family history.

BRA 14974; RC 15186

**"Everyday Use."** Alice Walker. In her *In Love and Trouble*, pp. 47-59. New York: Harcourt, Brace, Jovanovich, 1974. 138p. $2.65; In *Black-Eyed Susans: Classic Stories by and about Black Women*. Edited by Mary Washington. New York: Doubleday, 1975. 200p. $3.95.

This wonderful story about the generation gap is written from the perspective of an old woman whose eldest daughter is returning from the city for a visit. Her younger daughter, Maggie, lives at home and is shy and handicapped from a childhood fire. Dee's visit is full of surprises, as she appears in African dress with an Afro hairstyle and even a new (African) name. She studies her mother, takes photographs, and claims old family objects that she used to abhor. Both daughters want the old quilts, which Dee says Maggie will not appreciate. "She'd probably be backward enough to put them to

everyday use." The old woman and Maggie are happy when Dee returns to the city.
RD 06927

**"The Cost Depends on What You Reckon It In."** Joan Merrill Gerber. In her *Stop Here, My Friend*, pp. 15-31. Boston: Houghton-Mifflin Co., 1965. 271p.

Mrs. Shapiro visits her mother, Mrs. Weissberg, in Sherman's Rest Home three times a day, bringing her Jewish delicacies for her meals. Mrs. Weissberg, who speaks half in English and half in Yiddish, dislikes the home and preferred it at her daughter's house where she used to live. Mrs. Shapiro's guilt about keeping her mother in a home, and her juggling of her children and husband who do not even know of her daily visits, are sensitively depicted in this excellent story. The roles are somewhat reversed in *The Autobiography of My Mother* by Rosellen Brown (New York: Random House, 1976; Paper. New York: Ballantine Books, 1981). Gerda Stein, a 72-year-old civil rights lawyer who once defended Emma Goldman, finds that her daughter Renata and Renata's toddler daughter Tippy have moved in unexpectedly. Renata gives her mother the silent treatment, refuses to leave the apartment, and acts so strange that Gerda is worried about her grandchild. She takes them to the park to tell Renata that she will fight for custody of Tippy, but the child dies in an accident at the park. Three generations of females who cannot relate to each other are well depicted.

**All Our Tomorrows.** Josephine Lawrence. New York: Harcourt, 1959. 319p.

The dilemma of three women taking turns caring for their feisty elderly mother, as well as societal attitudes toward older people and the extended family, are presented in this novel. The first chapter (pp. 1-31) focuses on the situation of Roberta Kennard, 56. Her widowed 24-year-old daughter-in-law Allison and granddaughter Katy live with her and her husband, Howell. The problems of dealing with Mama, too, in this four-generation household are told from Roberta's point of view. This chapter can well be used as a basis for discussion.

Josephine Lawrence also wrote *Years Are So Long* (New York: Frederick A. Stokes Co., 1934) with a focus on Lucy and Barkley Cooper's call on their children for financial assistance, feeling it is their children's responsibility to care for them in their old age. But the five middle-aged children do not agree: "Our generation's duty isn't to the past; it's to the future. We're in debt to our children, not to you." The first chapter (pp. 1-28) is especially provocative, contrasting the values of the two generations as they discuss Barkley and Lucy's future.

Film. *Make Way for Tomorrow*. Paramount, 1937.

**"The Wonderful Old Gentleman."** Dorothy Parker. In *The Collected Stories of Dorothy Parker*, pp. 19-40. New York: New American Library, 1942. 362p.

Mr. and Mrs. Bain, and her sister Mrs. Whittaker, sit together while waiting for their father's death at age 84. Through their conversation, the reader gets a clear picture of a difficult, stingy old man who caused nothing but trouble for the poor Bains, with whom he lived, while he doted on wealthy Mrs. Whittaker.

TB 01985

**A Raisin in the Sun.** Lorraine Hansberry. New York: Random House, 1961. 113p. $1.95; Paper. New York: New American Library, 1961. $1.50.

In this play about a struggling black family, Mama (Leah Younger) is the central figure. She is expecting a $10,000 insurance check which she has earmarked for a new house and her children's careers. Her son, Walter, feels that he should be the head of their three-generation household. Although he loses the money his mama gives him, he finally "comes into his manhood" under her tutelage. Mama, in her mid-sixties, is a very strong matriarchal character in a classic black play.

BR 09977; RC 15750; Film. Columbia, 1961.

**"My Man, Bovanne."** Toni Cade Bambara. In her *Gorilla, My Love*. New York: Random House, 1972. 177p. $8.95; In *Black-Eyed Susans: Classic Stories by and about Black Women*, pp. 69-77. Edited by Mary Washington. New York: Doubleday, 1975. 200p. $3.95.

Mamma is at a dance for a political campaign her children support. They are scandalized at her relationship with Bovanne, "a nice ole gent from the block." She, in turn, is upset that Black Power has "got hold of their minds and mess them around." Although they want her at the party to represent "grass roots," they also want her to act according to their codes. Mamma is very aware of the generation gap in her family, but the children deny it.

RD 06094

**Of the Farm.** John Updike. New York: Knopf, 1965. 173p. $8.95; Paper. New York: Fawcett Book Group, 1981. $2.50.

Joe, with his new wife, Peggy, and her 11-year-old son, make the journey to his family farm. His earlier marriage, his career, the role of the farm in his life, are reflected in the intense dialogues with his aging mother, whose patterned game-playing Joe and Peggy work to foil. The ambivalence of the adult child's love for his older parent, and the stubborn will of his mother, provide the structure around which young Richard explores the world and Peggy discovers a new aspect of her husband's personality. The survival of all in this quartet gives a positive tone to the penetrating character study of four involved in the "problem of the aging parent."

BR 00220

**On Golden Pond.** Ernest Thompson. New York: Dodd, Mead, and Co., 1979. 191p. $7.95; Paper. New York: New American Library, 1981. $2.50.

Norman, 79, and his wife Ethel, 69, are at their summer home in Maine when their daughter Chelsea, 42, visits with her newest boyfriend, Bill, and his son, Billy. Chelsea and Norman have a tense relationship which she feels is based on his desire to have had a boy. Ethel and Norman have a very close, teasing, and warm marriage. Billy's stay at Golden Pond while Chelsea and Bill go to Europe leads to a close friendship between Norman and Billy, which in turn helps Chelsea's relationships with both. Norman's irascibility changes to warm appreciation of all his family. Light and funny, the play demonstrates many family and intergenerational relationships.

Film. United Artists, 1981.

**King Lear.** William Shakespeare.

Both King Lear and the Earl of Gloucester are "fourscore and upward," foolish and proud. This play features parallel stories about the two elders who are tricked into trusting their evil children and rejecting the devoted ones. Both rulers are deceived by appearances and inadvertently bring death to good people instead of bad.

BR 01082; BR 01525; TB 00348; Film. Columbia, 1970.

# INTERGENERATIONAL RELATIONSHIPS

With aging, one's intensive interaction with spouse and with close family changes as losses through maturing of children or death of spouse occurs. The strong long-term emotional attachments are not as regularly the substance of daily interaction, and the role of power in other people's lives may be transformed to a greater mutuality of exchange. The grandparent loves and nurtures without the ultimate responsibility; parent and adult son or daughter assume a new adult-to-adult relationship; there may be less sense of unity and more complementarity in most relationships. What is learned or exchanged across the intergenerational borders may rest more on acceptance and appreciation of others than on management and control of others. The elders see their own time and the future through young eyes, and the younger come to appreciate the significance of the past and now. This shift in daily social relationships becomes richly rewarding. Creative literature makes its contributions very importantly to understanding this area.

The "time-binding" role of the older adult with the generations that follow is greatly increased as the older person senses the urgency of interpreting the past and of traditions, and has a strong motive to tell the stories, convey the values, and assure the perpetuation of family and things he or she holds dear. And the children accept the tales as from another world and era. This is the ideal pattern, some of which is present in most intergenerational exchanges whether harmonious or abrasive.

**Successful Aging: The Facts and Fallacies of Growing Old.** Olga Knopf. New York: Viking Press, 1975. 229p. $8.95; Large Type. Boston: G. K. Hall, 1977. $12.50.

The aged parent and family relationships is one of a number of topics given important attention in this practical guide addressed to older adults as well as to the younger generation so that they may understand the physical and psychological aspects of aging.

**The Age Factor: Love, Sex and Friendship in Age Different Relationships.** Jack LaPatra. New York: M. Evans and Company/ Dutton, 1980. 214p. $9.95.

Readable, revealing interviews with "age-different" couples who have over 20 years difference in age. Age is seen as a relatively less significant factor than values, tastes, and stage of life in determining happy marriage and compatability. An interesting contrast to these happy marriages is Francoise Gilot's *Life with Picasso* (New York: McGraw-Hill Book Co., 1964) where an intimate relationship across the generations between the artist and his young French mistress led from her acceptance of Picasso, to worship, to disillusionment.

**Coming Home.** Shepard Ginades. New York: Delacorte Press, 1976. 222p.

How parents and grown children can confront each other more openly, communicate more freely, and become friends. Case studies and interviews with both parents and adult children on understanding and dealing with each other. Offers guidelines for both generations in preparation for a new adult-to-adult relationship.

**How to Grandparent.** Fitzhugh Dodson with Paula Reuben. New York: Harper & Row, 1981. 304p. $12.95.

Provides the basic understanding of child development that is a foundation for successful intergenerational relationship.

**Looking Ahead: A Woman's Guide to the Problems and Joys of Growing Older.** Edited by Lillian E. Troll and Joan and Kenneth Israel. New York: Prentice-Hall/Spectrum, 1977. 216p. $9.95; Paper $4.95.

Devotes a chapter to "Foster Grand-parenting."

**The Summer of the Great Grandmother.** Madeleine L'Engle. New York: Farrar, Straus, 1975. 245p. $10.95; Paper. New York: Seabury, 1980. $5.95.

Mutual respect, mutual forgiveness of old hurts, increased openness of exchange mark the relationship of the author to her dying mother and again to her son.

RC 09165

**Leavetaking: When and How to Say Goodbye.** Mortimer R. Feinberg and others. New York: Simon & Schuster, 1978. 286p.

Leavetaking is seen as a necessary human process throughout life, and ways of understanding and dealing with it are illuminated here. Loss of parents and departure of children from the home ("empty nest") are two intergenerational occasions for understanding this process.

## Creative Literature

**Harry and Tonto.** Josh Greenfield and Paul Mazursky. New York: Saturday Review Press, 1974. 183p.; Large Type. Boston: G. K. Hall, 1976.

When their apartment is demolished, Harry (a 72-year-old widower) and Tonto (his cat) take a cross-country trip visiting each of his adult children in turn. Along the way, they pick up a young woman hitchhiker; she and Harry become friends and share adventures. In the end Harry remains independent and alone.

BR 03131; RD 09037; Film. Fox, 1974.

**Kotch.** Katherine Topkins. New York: McGraw-Hill, 1965. 190p.

When Kotch's son and daughter-in-law decide that he should live in a retirement village rather than with them, he takes off. During his travels, he meets and befriends a pregnant teen-aged girl, Erica. They set up housekeeping together and he delivers her baby for her. At the end of this light-hearted novel, Kotch is reconciled with his son but continues to live independently.

Film. Cinerama, 1971.

**The Color of Evening.** Robert Nathan. New York: Knopf, 1960. 210p.

Max Loeb, an older painter, finds a young waif on the beach at Santa Monica and they fall in love. As they become involved, he realizes that she is better suited to his young pupil, and that he should turn to a woman his own age for companionship and affection.

**Harold and Maude.** Colin Higgins. New York: Avon Books, 1975. 145p. $1.95.

Another story of an intergenerational romance, this novel centers on Harold, 21, and Maude, 69, who evolve from friends to lovers. Harold is a loner whose only interests had been attending funerals and acting out suicides. Maude is the first real friend that he has ever had. Death and dying are major concerns of both characters in this blackly humorous story.

BR 01691; Film. Paramount, 1972.

**All the Little Live Things.** Wallace Stegner. Lincoln: University of Nebraska Press, 1979. 345p. $18.95; Paper $4.95.

Joe Allston and his wife, Ruth, both in their mid-sixties, move to California to retire. But their quiet life is interrupted by Jim Peck, a young man who starts a University of the Free Mind on their property. He reminds Joe of his recently deceased son, Curtis; their clashes appear to be based on unresolved father-son difficulties. Other disruptions include Tom Weld, who bulldozes the adjacent lot to develop it for resale, and Marian, a young new neighbor whose death marks them. The activities of the younger people contrasted with Joe's impulse to retreat into retirement make a most interesting account of intergenerational relationships.

BR 02291; TB 01865

**Mrs. Stevens Hears the Mermaids Singing.** May Sarton. New York: Norton, 1974. 240p. $6.95; Paper. New York: Norton, 1975. $3.95.

Mature Hilary Stevens' relationship with Mar, her young neighbor, provides the context for the novel. Hilary befriends Mar and comes to realize that her hopes for him as a poet are based on her earlier wish to be a boy. As a famous poet, she tries to serve as a critic of his writing, yet remain his friend in a difficult intergenerational relationship.

**The Old Man and the Sea.** Ernest Hemingway. New York: Charles Scribner's Sons, 1952. 140p. $12.50; Paper $3.25.

Hemingway's classic novella about a proud fisherman's battle with the sea is also a wonderful story of a friendship between generations. Santiago, the old fisherman, is friends with a young boy, Manolin, who understands his desperate struggle to get a fish after a streak of bad luck for 84 days.

BR 01600; RC 10319; RD 10319; Film. Warner Brothers, 1959.

**Balancing Acts.** Lynn Sharon Schwartz. New York: Harper & Row, 1981. 224p. $9.95; Paper 1982. $2.50; Large Type. South Yarmouth, Mass: John Curley and Associates, 1981. 390p.

Max Fried, a widower and ex-trapeze artist, at 76 teaches acrobatics to young people at the school, and Allison is his unusual pupil aged 13, sensitive, intellectually curious, well-read, and eager to know reality. This is the story of Allison's learning about independence and Max's learning about dependence. The balance needed in life, the interdependence of people, are the themes that emerge from a vital tale with an array of well-conceived characters, believable situations, and surprising developments.

**"Broken Homes."** William Trevor. In his *Lovers of Their Time and Other Stories*, pp. 7-26. New York: Viking Press, 1979. 279p. $10.95; Paper. New York: Penguin Books, 1980. $4.50.

A negative relationship between an older woman and the younger generation is depicted in this sad story. Mrs. Malby, 87, agrees to cooperate with a local school project to "foster a deeper understanding between generations" and allows a group of children from broken homes to paint her kitchen for her. Although she doesn't need her kitchen painted, she feels she must allow it; she is afraid that the reverend or the social worker will commit her to a nursing home if she appears senile or uncooperative. The values between generations clash, and the school experiment is a failure. Much food for thought and discussion.

BR 04331

**"The Warrior Princess Ozimba."** Reynolds Price. In *Stories of the Modern South*, pp. 309-314. Edited by Ben Forkner and Patrick Samway. New York: Penguin Books, 1981. 464p. $5.95; In *The Names and Faces of Heroes*. Edited by Reynolds Price. New York: Atheneum, 1973. $2.95.

A very short story about the Warrior Princess Ozimba, named after a character in a book, and her annual visit from the descendents of the family for whom she used to work. She is proud of the blue tennis shoes her former employer's great-grandson brings her each year, and of the respect the younger generation shows her.

RC 14436

**The Two of Us.** Claude Berri. New York: William Morrow Co., 1968. 156p.

Claude, at the age of nine, tells the story of his life with two elderly peasants, Pepe and Meme. He has been sent to stay with them during World War II so that his mischievousness will not attract the attention of the Nazis. Pepe is lovable and friendly but anti-semitic, a contradiction which the Jewish Claude must learn to understand. This novel and film portray a warm intergenerational friendship.

Film. Swank Motion Pictures Distributors, 1968.

**A Christmas Memory.** Truman Capote. New York: Random House, 1966. 45p. $12.95.

A 77-year-old woman and her 7-year-old cousin are best friends and allies. Every Christmas they bake fruitcakes for their friends and celebrate the holidays together. This charming novella is autobiographical as Capote lived with a distant elderly cousin himself until he was 10.

Film. *Truman Capote's Trilogy.* Allied Artists, 1969.

# COMPANIONSHIP AND FRIENDSHIP

As losses in family occur, older adults increasingly turn to friends for the companionship of shared living. The telephone becomes an important tool of regular communication, and coffee breaks, tea, or luncheon provide the occasion in middle-class America in which friendships are nourished. Joint projects—sports, hobbies, learning experiences, shared kitchen activities, activities at a community center—provide both an introduction to congenial folk and the occasion for developing a stronger friendship. Just as the intergenerational relationships become less controlling and more appreciative, so the substitution of friends for family requires a similar change in style.

Even family relationships undergo a transformation into friendship as years and personal maturity permit. Husband and wife relationships are intensified with the friendship factor, parent and adult child relationships mature into friendship, and so forth. The art of friendship is an art of aging.

The value of friends is not only in sociability but also in having a confidant. Research has documented that the availability of a confidant aids morale and mental stability during stressful periods of life. A great sense of loss may be felt at the death of a close, long-standing friend.

**The Friendship Factor.** Alan Loy McGinnis. Minneapolis: Augsburg Publishing House, 1979. 192p.

Friendship is characterized by intimacy, mutuality, and freedom, says McGinnis. Believing strongly in the rich rewards of friendship, the author presents a sensitive, perceptive analysis of the art of friendship in such chapters as "The Art of Self-Disclosure," "How to Communicate Warmth," and "The Art of Creative Forgiveness." Skilled counsel, extensively illustrated with pointed examples and relaxed humor, this book has a foundation of Christian values which emerge unobtrusively from time to time. This should have wide usefulness.

**Life Plans: Looking Forward to Retirement.** Grace W. Weinstein. New York: Holt, Rinehart and Winston, 1979. 252p. $9.95; Paper $4.95.

One of the major focus points of this informal, perceptive guide to retirement is "living in friendship."

**Looking Ahead: A Woman's Guide to the Problems and Joys of Growing Older.** Edited by Lillian E. Troll and Joan and Kenneth Israel. New York: Prentice-Hall/Spectrum, 1977. 216p. $9.95; Paper $4.95.

Readable and interesting insights into problems in human relations, family, sex, jobs, continuing education, and other matters. Two chapters are devoted to discussion of friendship, its role and its art.

**These Rich Years: A Journal of Retirement.** Jean and Robert Hersey. New York: Charles Scribner & Sons, 1969. 270p.

The blossoming of intensified friendship within the marriage relationship is one of the great rewards of retirement for the Herseys, who speak of it freely and record the stresses and resolutions within which this is achieved.

BRA 01516

**In the Fullness of Time.** Avis D. Carlson. South Bend, Ind.: Henry Regnery, 1977. 195p.; Large Type. South Yarmouth, Mass.: John Curley & Associates, 1979. $10.95.

Aware that "somebody needs to write from the inside about the experience of aging," Avis Carlson at the age of 80 pulled together the basic facts and set them in the framework of her own experience and those of friends and acquaintances. Friendship plays a strong role in her analysis, and is seen as one of the important forces in "maintaining a feeling of self-worth."

RD 11801

**Time on Our Hands: The Problem of Leisure.** Virginia Boyack and others. Los Angeles: Ethel Percy Andrus Gerontology Center, 1973. 73p.

The role of "sociability" and close relationships in maintaining health in aging. See especially pp. 14-18, 20.

**Friendship after Forty.** James Allen Sparks. Nashville: Abingdon Press, 1980. 144p. $7.95.

The value and importance of friends in the lives of middle-aged and older adults.

## Creative Literature

**"How Soon Can I Leave?"** Susan Hill. In *Solo: Women on Women Alone*, pp. 139-51. Edited by Linda and Leo Hamalian. New York: Dell, 1977. 367p. $1.95.

Miss Roscommon, an older woman of unspecified age, and Miss Bartlett, a middle-aged woman, live together "temporarily." Each feels that she is sharing her home out of charity to the other; neither can admit her own needs. The loneliness of the women is portrayed through an atmosphere of pent-up emotion and self-suffocation. After seven years, Miss Bartlett asserts her independence by moving out for a few months. Upon her return she discovers her friend's death, and her own loneliness.

**"Old Harry."** Josephine Johnson. In her *Winter Orchard*, pp. 85-103. New York: Simon & Schuster, 1935. 308p.

Pagsbrey and Old Harry have worked together as museum guards for ten years. They meet each day on the way in, and share their lunch hour. Pagsbrey is a retired Latin and Greek professor who lives in a boardinghouse; his friend Harry is uneducated and lives with his daughter and grandchildren, all of whom he supports. When Harry dies at the museum, Pagsbrey misses him terribly and discovers what real loneliness is. A poignant story, simply told.

**Diary of an Old Man.** Chaim Bermant. New York: Holt, Rinehart and Winston, 1967. 191p.

From February 12 to March 15 of his eighty-fourth year, Cyril keeps a diary. On the first day his young (74-year-old) friend Harry was buried; Cyril has only one close friend left, George. They go to the hospital together for their weekly treatments and share their pleasures—the park and the library. But in March, both George and Cyril's friendly landlady Mrs. Connachie die. Cyril is left without a home, and without a friend.

**Quartet in Autumn.** Barbara Pym. New York: Harper & Row, 1980. 218p. $2.50; Large Type. Boston: G. K. Hall, 1979. $10.95.

Four London clerks of retirement age become more concerned about each other as they each retire. Edwin, a widower with a daughter and grandchildren, sustains himself through his church activities. Norman lives in a "bed-sitter" and has only a brother-in-law as a social contact outside work. Marcia is alone in the world although she inherited a house; she becomes increasingly eccentric. Letty has one close friend and lives in a rented room. When the women retire, Edwin helps Letty resettle and Norman expresses concern for Marcia, who dies and leaves him her house. All four lead dreary, lonely lives with only the small concern of their officemates to help them.

BR 03903

**Waiting in the Wings.** Noel Coward. In *The Collected Plays of Noel Coward*, pp. 421-537. London: Heinemann, 1962.

This three-act play takes place in "The Wings," a small charity home for retired actresses. The nine women who live there are friends and have a pleasant relationship with the manager, Miss Archie, and the Wings committee secretary, Perry Lascoe. But the tranquillity is destroyed when Lotta Bainbridge moves in. She and another resident, May Davenport, both in their seventies, have a 30-year-old animosity over a mutual beau who married Lotta. By the end of the play, they have resolved their difficulties and become friends again.

**"The Flight of Betsey Lane."** Sarah Orne Jewett. In her *The Country of the Pointed Firs and Other Stories*. Garden City, N.Y.: Doubleday, 1954. 320p. $2.95.

A portrait of three elderly women living at Byfleet Poorhouse, this story illustrates the friendships developed among the residents who enjoy living at the town's farm during the winter.

RC 16145

**Apostles of Light.** Ellen Douglas. Boston: Houghton Mifflin, 1973. 307p.

When the house of his lifelong lover Martha is turned into a nursing home, Lucas Alexander moves in. He is pleased to be able to live near her and spend so much time with her. Also, as a retired doctor, he can help her with her arteriosclerosis and the other patients with their ailments. A loyal and loving friend, he tries to help Martha and the others against the evil administrator, Howie. When he feels that he can save them in no other way, Lucas sets fire to the house. A melodramatic ending to an excellent novel.

RD 07313

**"Where the Cloud Breaks."** H. E. Bates. In *The Best of H. E. Bates*, pp. 414-25. Boston: Little, Brown and Co., 1963. 454p.

Colonel Gracie, an old man of unstated age, lives by himself and is becoming senile. He has missed his friend and neighbor, Miss

Wilkinson, 60, who has been away. She has now invited him for tea and he's very excited about seeing her again. "He felt a sort of whisper travel across his heart" but he was too shy to confess his feelings for her. The long friendship of these lonely people is threatened by the arrival of a third party, Miss Wilkinson's television set. A very well-written story.

# SEXUALITY

The myth that sexual interest dies with the arrival of the sixties has now expired, and the stereotype of the elderly population as nonsexual is beginning to be replaced by a reasonable acceptance of sexuality as a continuingly important aspect of life for many well into their eighties and nineties. Open discussion of sexuality in later years has become important in developing acceptance of new modes of behavior, and fiction plays an important role in modeling the "new" older adult. The problems of health and waning vigor, however, must be frankly faced, and physicians and psychologists too have turned their attention to sexuality as a vital force in giving interest and meaning to life in the later years.

**The Fires of Autumn: Sexual Activity in the Middle and Later Years.**
Peter Q. Dickinson. New York: Drake Publishers, Inc., 1974. 192p.; Paper. New York: Sterling Publisher, 1977. $4.95.

Accepting sexual drives as fundamental to human well-being throughout life, Dickinson provides a useful illumination of how these were dealt with in other times and cultures before he details our current orientation to sex and to sex in the older years. He deals with the life phases' influence on sex through the female menopause and discusses the relationship of heart attacks, strokes, prostate surgery, and various other illnesses to the exercise of sexual needs. Recognizing the need in older years for increased stimulation, Dickinson presents the possibilities of physical experimentation and even of the use of pornography by those to whom these more extreme variations from tradition may have appeal. Threesomes, community living and group marriages as innovative styles are objectively reported for their potential for older adults. Wide range of alternatives that may shock some and for others may provide frank analysis and understanding. This volume was one of the early frank explorations that helped to explode the myth that adults are sexless after 65.

Other books related to this subject include: *Sex after Sixty: A Guide for Men and Women for Their Later Years* by Robert N. Butler and Myrna I. Lewis (New York: Harper & Row, 1976; Large Type. Boston: G. K. Hall, 1977. BR 03108); *Sex in Later Life* by Ivor Felstein (New York: Penguin Books, 1974); *Love in the Later Years: The Emotional, Physical, Sexual, and Social Potential of the Elderly* by James A. Peterson and Barbara Payne (New York: Association Press, 1975); *Sex and the Aging Heart* by Lee Scheingold and Nathaniel Wagner (New York: Jove Publishing Group, 1975); and *Use It or You'll Lose It: You're Never Too Old to Enjoy Sex—Here's How and Why* by Joseph S. Poticha (New York: Marek, 1978).

## Creative Literature

**The Color of Evening.** Robert Nathan. New York: Knopf, 1960. 210p.

Max Loeb is a painter using Mrs. Bloemendal's garage as a studio. His only pupil is a young man, Jon, who becomes his rival for a young girl they meet on the beach. Halys is a homeless waif who feels that she is in love with Max when he takes her into his home. Mrs. Bloemendal is jealous, as is Jon. Max finds that a long-lost feeling returns to him about Halys. Chapter 11 (pp. 127-37) describes their romance at its peak. Good for group reading and discussion.

**The Chrysanthemum Garden.** Joseph Cowley. New York: Simon & Schuster, 1981. 172p. $11.95.

Morna Franklin reviews her life with Denny McArdle, who has recently died at 82. She met him in middle age when she took a class from him at the New School; their affair has continued ever since. The sexual aspect of their relationship is implicit.

**A Thousand Summers.** Garson Kanin. Garden City, N.Y.: Doubleday, 1973. 246p.; Large Type. Boston: G. K. Hall, 1973.

Written from the vantage point of Mr. Osborn, this portrays a middle-aged couple's love affair that continues until they are in their sixties. Osborn met Sheila van Anda when he was 34 and they were both married. World War II intervened, but they remained lovers until her death. The sexual aspect of their relationship is understated but clear. Osborn is now 79 and a resident at Falmouth Sunset House; this is his memory.

RD 06863

**Diary of a Mad Old Man.** Junchiro Tanizaki. New York: Knopf, 1965. 177p.; Paper. New York: Putnam, 1981. $5.95.

Utsugi, 77, retains his sexual urges despite a stroke. Although he is impotent, he is excited by his daughter-in-law Satsuko whom he goads into an intimate relationship with him and into an affair with his nephew. Utsugi is aroused by the knowledge of her affair and enjoys the turmoil he has created in his own household. After a second stroke the doctor warns Satsuko against exciting her father-in-law; Utsugi's final remaining sexual pleasure is looking at the rubbings he has made of Satsuko's feet.

**Travels with My Aunt.** Graham Greene. New York: Viking Press, 1970. 244p. $14.95; Paper. New York: Penguin Books, 1979. $2.95.

Seventy-five-year-old Augusta Bertram takes her nephew Henry on a whirlwind international trip in search of her true love in Paraguay. As she tells Henry of her earlier exploits and loves, her continuing sexual activity is clearly hinted at. Her personal servant is also her lover, but is sacrificed to her long lost Paraguayan love and partner in crime. Delightfully eccentric and bracing.

BR 01253; RD 14936; Film. Metro-Goldwyn-Mayer, 1972.

**After Many a Summer Dies the Swan.** Aldous Huxley. New York: Harper & Row, 1965. 246p.

Despite his great wealth, Jo Stoyte, in his eighties, finds his greatest pleasure in his sexual relationship with his mistress, Virginia, some 60 years younger than he. In order to continue his sexual life, he receives injections of testosterone and sponsors research into longevity. Humorous satire with startling ending.

RC 12182

**"The Story of the Old Man and the Pretty Girl."** Italo Svevo. In his *Short Sentimental Journey and Other Stories*, pp. 71-128. Berkeley: University of California Press, 1967. 319p. $21.50.

An old man (unnamed) has an affair with a 20-year-old pretty girl (unnamed) whom he meets on the trolley. He tries to convince himself that the affair is good for his heart and that his presence is instructive to the girl. But he is ambivalent about their relationship and shifts between being romantic and being avuncular with her. At the end he dies while writing in his journal about morality and sexuality in old age.

# LIFE REVIEW

Looking back, reminiscing, using memories for enjoyment, for instruction of the young, or for restoration of self-esteem is a common experience among older adults. This is one aspect of life review.

There is a second aspect of life review that is more profound in the energy it uses and in the impact on personality. At major turning points of our mature lives (new careers, retirement, loss of spouse, approaching death) we tend to respond to the challenge of these basic changes by reviewing our past lives, by putting our past lives into a perspective that incorporates the new event. People in the later years of life, challenged as they are by role losses, by death of family and friends, by changes in living arrangements, find life review a major task. We must maintain continuity with the past, we must integrate these later stages of life into our perception of ourselves, and we must understand the past in the light of these new situations.

Concurrent with this task of life review, adults facing death find it important to weigh and judge themselves by more stringent standards than they may have applied before. We find it important to review the old unresolved problems and relationships that need repair, to "put the house in order."

Life review at these three levels is a normal, productive process, according to Robert N. Butler, psychiatrist. To be sure, any of these impulses and processes can be abused by the older person: unwanted garrulousness in reminiscing that dominates conversations and people; depression and self-flagellation in reassessing one's life; buying the restoration of relationships through gifts of money and promised bequests. But the function of life review well-used leads to insights, personal growth, and the achievement of new levels of wisdom and serenity.

**Passages: The Predictable Crises of Adult Life.** Gail Sheehy. New York: Dutton, 1976. 393p.; Paper. New York: Bantam Books, 1977. $3.95.

Taken from the middle class lives of America's "pacesetter group," the series of life crises from the age of 20 to the age of 55 discussed here will trigger recall by many in our society and stimulate a life review process. Sheehy recognizes that each life phase brings its own demands and pressures to conform, behind which and through which individual personality must struggle to emerge. Extensive case illustrations are drawn from the 115 life histories she developed through personal interview. The book's bestseller status speaks for its capacity to address the interests and concerns of many people.

RD 09919

**The Three Boxes of Life: And How to Get Out of Them: An Introduction to Life/Work Planning.** Richard Nelson Bolles. Berkeley, Calif.: Ten Speed Press, 1978. 416p. $19.95; Paper $8.95.

Proposes a time-line construction of major decisions in one's life, with recall exercises (remember faces, voices, scenes, events, etc.) around each point, together with "write it, tell it, draw it" exercises. Useful initial group introduction to life review. See especially pp. 358-61, "The Life Review."

**Growing Older: The Things You Need to Know about Aging.** Margaret Hellie Huyck. New York: Prentice-Hall, 1974. 179p.

This highly empathetic volume on aging covers many aspects of this stage of life. A four-page section (pp. 160-63) deals with accepting the consequences of choices made.

BRA 14133; RC 09137

**On Death and Dying.** Elisabeth Kübler-Ross. New York: Macmillan, 1969. 260p.

"Therapy with the Terminally Ill" (chapter 13) describes the confessions or "making arrangements" of dying patients as they prepare themselves for death and attain the feeling of peace.

BRA 14168; RD 06132

**The End of Senility.** Arthur S. Freese. New York: Arbor House, 1978. 178p. $8.95; Large Type. South Yarmouth, Mass.: John Curley & Associates, 1979. $8.95.

A brief discussion of "life review therapy" focuses on the verbal autobiography by way of memories and memorabilia to bring out past emotional experiences for better self-understanding, resolving of old conflicts, and settling of old problems.

RC 13576

"The Life Review: An Interpretation of Reminiscence in the Aged" by Robert N. Butler (in Robert Kastenbaum's *New Thoughts on Old Age* [New York: Springer Publishing Co., 1964], pp. 265-80) provides Butler's classic statement of the process and significance of life review, for those who wish to probe more deeply.

**Write the Story of Your Life.** Ruth Kanin. New York: Elsevier/ Dutton, 1981. 219p. $15.50; Paper $9.95.

This "how-to-do-it" manual provides a guide to focused reminiscence for those who want to "put it all together." In the early stages of recall and self-acceptance there are exercises useful even for those not planning to write a full life review. On the other hand, there is also guidance to formats of different lengths and structures (memoirs, portraits, confessions, short stories, etc.) and advice on critiquing one's own manuscript. Excellent bibliographies accompany this first-rate text on how to write an autobiography, imparting self-confidence and personal recognition along the way.

**Bi-Folkal Media Kits for Older Adults.** Lynne Martin Erickson and Kathryn Leide. Blue Mounds, Wis.: Bi-Folkal Productions, Inc.

A series of kits containing slide-tape programs, cassettes of related music, touch-smell-do equipment for group activities on a series of topics that will stimulate pleasant recall in older adults: Remembering the Depression, Remembering Train Rides, Remembering Birthdays, Remembering Automobiles, Remembering 1924, and so on. The ten or more kits were priced between $125 and $150 in 1981. Manuals accompany each kit. A slide tape on developing your own programs is included for public librarians, for activity directors in senior centers, day care centers for older adults, or nursing homes.

A comparable series by Kathy Coster and Barbara Webb (Baltimore County Public Library) is often built around one of the Bi-Folkal Kits: *Gray and Growing: Program Packages for the Older Adult: A Manual* (1978).

**Until the Singing Stops: A Celebration of Life and Old Age in America.** Don Gold. New York: Holt, Rinehart and Winston, 1979. 352p. $12.50.

Oral histories of a group of 20 older men and women with the focus on life review. Each will stimulate readers to recall their own lives. For individual reading or group oral reading and reminiscence. RC 15013

**We Didn't Have Much but We Sure Had Plenty: Stories of Rural Women.** Sherry Thomas. Garden City, N.Y.: Doubleday Publishing Co., 1981. 208p. $7.95.

In documentary form, simple stories of everyday people and their ordinary lives in the early part of this century. Typical oral history in book form.

## LIFE REVIEW IN FORMAL BIOGRAPHY

**Markings.** Dag Hammarskjold. New York: Alfred Knopf, 1964. 186p. $11.95; Paper. Lawrence, Mass.: Merrimack Book Service, 1966; Large Type. Boston: G. K. Hall, 1976.

Journal kept by the retired head of the United Nations, reflecting on his life and indicating spiritual growth, together with premonitions of his death. A moving spiritual record.

BR 00042; CB 00854; TB 00854

**A Personal Geography.** Elizabeth Coatsworth. Brattleboro, Vt: Stephen Greene Press, 1976. 192p. $9.95; Large Type. Boston: G. K. Hall, 1979. $9.95.

These selections from the private journal of a talented writer cover her experiences and insights from youth to old age. The book ends with provocative comments on the changing quality and expectations of life as a person ages. As she states in the preface: "Outwardly, I am 83 years old, but inwardly I am every age, embodying the emotions and experiences of every period of my growth."

RD 10257

**All the Strange Hours: The Excavation of a Life.** Loren Eiseley. New York: Charles Scribner's Sons, 1975. 273p. $4.95; Encore Edition $3.95.

Eiseley's life, from his painful childhood in Nebraska, through his drifter period of adolescence and many other physical and mental vicissitudes, could hardly have been forecasted to become that of a scientific philosopher. Hard fact and pure poetry combine in his search for the meaning of life.

RC 16183

**Small World, Long Gone.** Avis Carlson. Chicago: Chicago Review Press, 1977. 195p. $7.95; Large Type. South Yarmouth, Mass.: John Curley & Associates, 1979. $9.95.

Carlson recalls the Dungans and the Halls as she knew them growing up in southern Kansas. "Not until much later did I realize my luck in growing up among the voluble, dogmatic, contentious Dungans. They all had bone-deep integrity. Not one of them was a liar or a cheat. Not one of them would ever refuse to lend a hand to a neighbor in trouble." "Where the Dungans read and argued, the Halls sang and joked." Grandparents, aunts, uncles remembered and treasured.

Sd-BPH (CB-1751) RC

**Such a Life.** Edith LaZebnik. New York: William Morrow, 1978. 287p. $8.95; Large Type. Boston: G. K. Hall, 1979. $13.95.

Written as flowingly as a chatty novel, Edith LaZebnik's autobiography is a rich, warm recounting of her parents' life and her own, told with a delightful Yiddish accent. Realistic rather than romantic in orientation, although young love and marriage have been highlighted, with attacks by Cossaks and Poles, and the inevitable traumas of grief and death as counterpoint to the evolving life of a vigorous, good-humored, insightful woman overflowing with zest. Will elicit life review for those with parallel life patterns that end with migration to the United States.

**Journal of a Solitude, 1970-1971.** May Sarton. New York: W. W. Norton, 1973. 208p. $11.95; Paper 1977. $3.95; Large Type. Boston: G. K. Hall, 1977. $13.95.

A chief volume of the series which shares May Sarton's daily journal with her readers over a span of a dozen years or more as Sarton goes through major mid-life adjustments and changes, and as she approaches aging through her own experience and that of a multitude of close friends. Sensitive, open, self-examining, honest.

Nj-B (C1472m) RC

Her *The House by the Sea* (New York; W. W. Norton, 1981) develops the themes even further.

BRA 16011; Me-BPH (MEC 80) RC

**The Measure of My Days.** Florida Scott-Maxwell. New York: Knopf, 1968. 150p.; Paper. New York: Penguin Books, 1979. $3.95.

"I was astonished to find out how intensely one lives in one's eighties. The last years seemed a culmination and by concentrating on them one became more truly oneself." Writing from the vantage point of her eighties, Scott-Maxwell reflects her new perspective on her years. Intelligent, perceptive, a lady shares the burning insights of the end of life.

**The Dialogues of Archibald MacLeish and Mark Van Doren.** Edited by Warren V. Bush. New York: E. P. Dutton, Inc., 1964. 285p.

For three days MacLeish and Van Doren visited at the MacLeish farm in Massachusetts, walking, swimming, relaxing in the music room, talking all the time—about being a writer, about the law (which MacLeish had studied at Harvard), about teaching (which Van Doren had done for a lifetime at Columbia), about freedom, art, friendship, God, and about their mutual friends (persons of some distinction). They were often putting their reminiscences into new perspective in their exchange; they were being creative in the fresh viewpoints that recall in their seventies gave to experiences of their twenties or their forties. Delightful, civilized, informal, and interesting conversation to sit in on! An hour of these dialogues were televised in 1962.

# AUTOBIOGRAPHIES THAT REFLECT OUR TIMES

**Baruch, My Own Story.** Bernard M. Baruch. New York: Holt, Rinehart and Winston, 1957. 337p.

From the Reconstruction to the splitting of the atom, Baruch reviews his 87 years as a balance of change and continuity. "None of us really outgrows his childhood. How we meet problems of adult life usually does not differ greatly from how we met the problems of growing up."
BRA 10296

**I Remember It Well.** Maurice Chevalier. New York: Macmillan, 1970. 221p.

In brief diary-like entries Chevalier's reminiscences are interspersed with his meditations on age, death, recollections of his mother, his early days, and the state of the world in his day.
BRA 05012

**The Right Time: An Autobiography.** Harry Lewis Golden. New York: Putnam, 1969. 450p. $6.95.

With wit and compassion, Golden presents reminiscences with anecdotes and vignettes of his Jewish boyhood, his marriage to an Irish Catholic girl, his many business ventures, his editorship of the

*Carolina Israelite*, and his friendship with notables. Zestful and enjoyable.

**Myself among Others.** Ruth Gordon. New York: Atheneum Publishers, 1971. 389p. $10.00.

An actress who made her stage debut in 1915 with Maude Adams in *Peter Pan* and a writer who has become a public favorite as an aging raconteur, Gordon recounts her life and friendships.

TB 03974

**On Reflection: An Autobiography.** Helen Hayes and Sandford Doty. Philadelphia: J. B. Lippincott, 1968. 256p. $8.95.

The autobiography that the famous actress wrote as a legacy for her grandchildren.

BRA 03612; TB 02511

**An Unfinished Woman: A Memoir.** Lillian Hellman. Boston: Little, Brown, 1970. 280p. $11.95; Paper. New York: Bantam Books, 1974. $2.75.

The first in a series of self-portraits with friends, a later title being *Pentimento*. Unsentimental, honest, sometimes with unusual penetration, this draws from memory and diaries to share the highlights of her life: the Spanish Civil War, the McCarthy era, and her liaison with Dashiell Hammett, perhaps the most meaningful of all.

TB 02924

**Autobiography of Values.** Charles A. Lindbergh. New York: Harcourt, Brace, Jovanovich, 1978. 423p.

A life review with focus not only on the public events of his life but also on his values as a boy and their evolution as he grew older.

RD 11230

**Blackberry Winter: My Earlier Years.** Margaret Mead. New York: William Morrow, 1972. 305p. $11.95; Paper 1973. $3.95.

The anthropologist describes her early life in a happy three-generational household, her student days at Barnard College, her research in the South Seas, her three marriages, and her experiences as mother and grandmother. Not only a reflection of the world around her but her unique personal values and orientations and their evolution.

RD 06409

**The Night We Stopped the Trolley.** Earl Schenck Miers. New York: Four Winds Press, 1969. 128p.

Reminiscences of childhood and youth in Brooklyn and Hackensack, New Jersey, during World War I and in the 1920s and 1930s. Recounted with humor and gusto, the life of this writer is viewed with nostalgia for the simplicities and wholesome living.

**The Land Remembers: The Story of a Farm and Its People.** Ben Logan. New York: Viking Press, 1975. 320p. $11.95; Paper. New York: Avon Books, 1976. $1.75; Large Type. Boston: G. K. Hall, 1976. $13.50.

The story of the farm is the story of the Logans, the growing up of the children and the maturing of their parents, their love of the land and of each other. The fury of the storm, the discovery of the bee tree, and a multitude of other farm events shape the direction of their lives. This is a life remembered by one of the sons.

RD 08318

Ben Logan treasures the development of memories, and in his novel *The Empty Meadow* (Madison, Wis.: Stanton & Lee Publishers, 1983) 17-year-old Steve peoples his "empty meadow" with shadows that will never go away. For those who approach 17 and for those who want to remember.

**When I Was Old.** Georges Simenon. New York: Harcourt, Brace, Jovanovich, 1971. 343p.

An autobiographical journal that is a self-exploration of what makes the author tick. Reflects his total commitment to his wife and children and his involvement in their daily lives. Sensitive sharing of life review.

**Maybe.** Lillian Hellman. Boston: Little, Brown and Company, 1980. 106p. $9.95; Paper 1982. $4.95.

Ambiguous and enigmatic as life, this is a memoir, or maybe a novel. Lillian Hellman recalls what she knew of the elusive and beautiful Sarah Cameron and her husband Carter, in the bits of contact over the years. Each stage of her recall casts new light on the mysterious Sarah and her death. In the end, with a horror suggested in an ultracivilized conversation, Lillian decides that while she'll never truly understand, maybe she has grasped the kernel ... maybe.

RC 16851

## Creative Literature

**"Sex Education."** Dorothy Canfield. In *The Experience of the American Woman*, pp. 195-206. Edited by B. H. Solomon. New York: New American Library, 1978. 450p. $2.95.

A single incident involving Malcolm, a young minister, is recounted by Aunt Minnie three times. She recalls the episode when she is in her thirties, in her fifties, and in her eighties — and gains a new perspective each time.

**The Will of Magda Townsend.** Margaret Culkin Banning. New York: Harper & Row, 1974. 318p.; Large Type. Boston: G. K. Hall, 1974.

Magda Townsend, a famous author of 35 novels, decides to rewrite her will when she turns 80. It is 28 years since her last will and much has changed in her family of two children and seven grandchildren. While writing her will, she reviews her life and her relationships. She also philosophizes about wills and their purposes — prophecy, bribery, communication — and decides to use hers only to give her family loving going-away presents from her.
RD 07228

**"Asphodel, That Greeny Flower."** William Carlos Williams. In his *Pictures from Breughel: Collected Poems 1950-1962*, pp. 153-82. New York: New Directions, 1967. 184p. $4.95.

The poet wrote this love poem to his wife in old age. He recalls their life together and their long love. "As I think of it now/after a lifetime, it is as if/a sweet-scented flower/were poised/and for me did open."

**The Stone Angel.** Margaret Laurence. New York: Bantam Books, 1981. 304p. $2.95; Large Type. London, Ont.: Gatefold Ltd., 1964.

Hagar Shipley, 90, is "rampant with memory." The novel follows her reminiscences from her childhood through her adult life to the present. The reader admires Hagar's courage and determination, yet she is not a completely sympathetic character — she is unyielding, proud, hypercritical of her children, and unable to show love to her family. Her life in Manawaka, a pioneer town, is an interesting one for her to review and the reader to experience.
BRA 03038

**The Spectator Bird.** Wallace Stegner. New York: Doubleday, 1976. 240p. $6.95; Paper. Lincoln: University of Nebraska Press, 1979. $3.50; Large Type. Boston: G. K. Hall, 1977.

A postcard from an old acquaintance in Denmark triggers a life review for Joe Allston, a retired literary agent in his late sixties. He shares with his wife Ruth a secret journal he'd kept 20 years before when they were in Denmark. The history of their friend, and the tales of their trip are fascinating, but the real story in this National Book Award novel is Joe's perspective on his life. There's also a good discussable section on societal attitudes toward aging (pp. 116-21).

BR 03759

**Recapitulation.** Wallace Stegner. New York: Doubleday, 1979. 278p. $8.95.

A lifetime of memories wash over Bruce Mason during a two-day visit to Salt Lake City after a 45-year absence. Returning to bury his Aunt Margaret, he has thought to see his best friend from teen-aged days, but decides that the relationship doesn't exist anymore except as part of his ever-present past. Another Stegner novel which focuses on life review.

**"Lullabye."** Leslie Sieko. In *The Best American Short Stories 1975*, pp. 254-63. Edited by Martha Foley. Boston: Houghton Mifflin, 1975. 340p.

Poignant and sad, this is the story of an old Navajo woman, Ayah, waiting for her husband Chato to leave the bar where he is spending their welfare check. She reminisces about her children, all of whom are dead or gone, and the problems her family has had assimilating into the white society. She is alone now with Chato from whom she feels estranged, and "her life has become memories."

**A Woman of Independent Means.** Elizabeth Forsythe Hailey. New York: Viking Press, 1978. 256p. $10.95; Paper. New York: Avon Books, 1979. $2.50; Large Type. Boston: G. K. Hall, 1979. $17.50.

From her first letter, written when she was 9 in 1899, to her last in 1968, Elizabeth Alcott's life story is told through her correspondence. Her writing portrays a strong, egoistic, generous, and exuberant woman who enjoyed her adventures. The last 38 pages of the novel deal with her life from age 55 to 78 years, and can stand alone for reading and discussion if an explanation of people's names is given.

RC 13255

**Praise the Human Season.** Don Robertson. New York: Ballantine
    Books, 1975. 640p. $1.95.
    Although they are both ill, Howard Amberson, 74, decides that
he and his wife Anne, 72, should take an automobile trip to seek the
secret of life. Just before their trip, Howard starts a journal which he
continues during their journey. In it he reviews their life together; the
novel alternates between his entries and the present tense. The
reviewers called this a humorous love story—it does concentrate on
Howard and Anne's long and loving relationship.
    RC 11372

**Perilous Voyage.** Lael Wertenbaker. Boston: Little, Brown and Co.,
    1975. 262p.
    When her doctors and relatives refuse to let Augusta MacGregor
Turnley die, although she is completely paralyzed, she decides to use
her time and isolation to review her past. She is proud of her
independent spirit which she recalls in vivid flashes of her life.
    RC 08953

**Goodbye, Mr. Chips.** James Hilton. New York: Bantam Books,
    1969. 125p. $1.95.
    Eighty-five-year-old Mr. Chipping (known to his students as Mr.
Chips) reminisces about his life and career as headmaster at
Brookfield School in this popular novel.
    BR 00528; RC 10974; RD 10974; TB 02018; Film. MGM, 1969.

**Good Morning, Midnight.** Jean Rhys. New York: Random House,
    1974. 159p. $2.95.
    Sasha Jansen tells the story of her life as she recalls it during a
visit to Paris, where she'd lived and worked as a young woman. Now
old, her past leaps at her in every restaurant and street. She relives her
past while remembering the husband who deserted her and the baby
she lost many years before. A sad, poignant story of a lonely woman.

**"What Happens Next?"** Gilbert Rogin. In *Jewish-American Stories*,
    pp. 122-28. Edited by Irving Howe. New York: New American
    Library, 1977. 470p. $2.50.
    When Julian decides to write about his 69-year-old father, he
interviews him to learn about his life. There is humor in the father's
self-deception and meaning in his memories.

**The Autobiography of Miss Jane Pittman.** Ernest J. Gaines. New
   York: Dial Press, 1971. 245p. $8.95; Paper. New York: Bantam
   Books, 1972. $2.25; Large Type. Boston: G. K. Hall, 1976.
   $10.95.
A student spends eight to nine months interviewing Miss Jane
Pittman, a black woman over 100 years old. She reviews her life from
the Civil War (Book I) through Reconstruction (II), Plantation life
(III), to the Civil Rights Movement (IV).
   BR 01645; CB 00391; RC 16542; Film. CBS, 1974.

**"The Jolly Corner."** Henry James. In *The American Short Story*,
   pp. 82-115. Edited by Calvin Skaggs. New York: Dell, 1977.
Spencer Brydon, 56, returns to New York after living in England
for 33 years. He asks himself: "What would America have made of
him? How would living in New York have changed his life?" He
discovers a ghost in his old family home; it is his other, American,
self. He reaches a psychological crisis when he meets the ghost. A
subplot concerns Alice Staverton, an old girlfriend who still loves him,
and his effort to regain his past through her. The National
Endowment for the Humanities American Short Story Series included
this story. Available in many anthologies and editions.
   Film. Perspective, 1977.

# HEALTH

Health and a sense of being in good health provide a foundation
upon which the sense of well-being rests. For most people in our
society, health is assumed as a given, and the capacity to cultivate a
sense of well-being when in ill health is a learned capacity. Most older
adults strive to maintain health (through proper diet, exercise,
avoidance of disease and catastrophic accident, etc.) and find the
concern for mental health (freedom from depression, anxiety, stress,
with maintenance of zest) closely connected with physical well-being.
   Although "nobody ever died of old age," as Sharon Curtin
phrases it, aging is usually accompanied by loss of powers (sight,
hearing, muscle tone, memory) and by breakdowns or disease in one
or more of the body's systems. Postponing and then coping with these
losses and limitations, whether minor or major, is part of the
experience of aging. Cardiovascular problems, diabetes, cancer, and
nervous system disorders each set their own limits to the range of
activities and to the sense of well-being. Rapid medical advances in

treatment and in prevention of major disorders associated with aging have been a prime cause of our rise in life expectancy, so that women of 65 years of age may expect to live to 82, while men of 65 may expect to live to 78. Longevity and rejuvenation are matters of basic health science as well as of fads and quackery.

The results of research on mental health and its links to physical health are gradually incorporated into laymen's literature and common practice. The role of exercise and diet in later years has attained a major importance in maintenance of mental as well as physical health programs.

Preoccupation with health problems, however, can be boring to others, and shuts off opportunities for commitment and expanding contacts in new and exciting areas of life. As aging takes an inevitable toll in bodily problems, the capacity to rise above these problems, to ignore them once they are prescribed for and dealt with, to attain what some call "body transcendence," is a mark of wisdom and maturity which many older adults are able to achieve. The goal in the proper concern for health is zestful living!

**Over 55: A Handbook on Health.** Edited by Theodore G. Duncan. Philadelphia: Franklin Institute Press, 1982. 633p. $27.50.

Drawing on the expertise of some 50 specialists (primarily medical and health experts on the staff of Pennsylvania Hospital), Dr. Duncan has organized a well-written, indexed manual for the layman on the common health concerns and diseases associated with the elderly. The detail on anatomy, the effects of specific disorders, typical treatment and prognosis, make this both an informative and reassuring source of understanding. Arthritis, bone, heart, and circulatory diseases, kidney and neurological disease, gastrointestinal disorders, cancer, gynecological problems, eye, skin, throat, teeth, and foot problems are covered.

Advice on diet, physical fitness, sexual activity, plastic surgery, and coping with crisis is given. Background information on population trends, nursing homes, hospitals, hospice care, insurance, retirement incomes, fraud, and funerals conclude this enormously informative, authoritative handbook.

**Nobody Ever Died of Old Age.** Sharon R. Curtin. Boston: Little, Brown and Company, 1973. 228p. $8.95; Paper $4.95; Large Type. Boston: G. K. Hall, 1973. 270p.

Identifies the social attitudes that shelve the elderly and depersonalize them both in institutional and community living as the chief source of ill health among the elderly. Compassionate, angry, humane telling of the stories of a group of American elderly, with suggestions for organizing and activating reform to rescue sanity and mental health, upon which all health depends.

    RD 06375; Film (16mm). Wilmette, Ill.: Films Inc., 1977.

**The View from Eighty.** Malcolm Cowley. New York: Viking Press, 1980. 96p. $6.95; Paper. New York: Penguin Books, 1982. $3.95; Large Type. Boston: G. K. Hall, 1981. $9.95.

    Candid presentation of the reality of being 80, when the "signals from the body" tell us we are old, but—given a sense of purpose and maintenance of some kind of involvement with life—these body signals inhibit vigorous living surprisingly little. Delightfully written.

    BR 04729; FD 15814; RC 15814

**The End of Senility.** Arthur S. Freese. New York: Arbor House, 1978. 178p. $8.95; Large Type. South Yarmouth, Mass.: John Curley & Associates, 1979. $8.95.

    Stereotypical "old age" and its myths are here revised in the light of research findings, and the case is made that "more years do not mean less life." Acknowledging the negative effect of society's ageism, Dr. Freese presents the scientific base for declaring that "senility is obsolete" and that, lacking specific diseases, aging need not make drastic reversals in life activity and enjoyment. Highly informed discussion of sexuality and mental and emotional health, with sound advice on norms and the expected range in behavior. Detailed analysis of the causes and treatment of depression and suicidal tendencies; problems in the use of drugs and alcohol; problems in diet—all are discussed frankly. Sources of information and help are listed. A manual on health for the mature adult wanting a preventive health program, or for the middle-aged adult helping an aging parent.

    RC 13576

**The Truth about Senility: How to Avoid It.** Lawrence Galton. New York: Thomas Y. Crowell, 1979. 244p. $9.95.

    Symptoms of cardiovascular problems, the phenomenon of depression, nutritional deficiencies are seen as commonly confused with "senility." Drugs, diet, exercise, or surgery are explored for their contributions to control or elimination of each of the particular problems. For the intelligent layperson eager to understand "what it is" and "what can be done." Orientation to the fast-growing medical specialization of geriatrics.

RD 13944

For greater detail on brain structure and function in lay terms, Robin M. Henig's *The Myth of Senility: Misconceptions about the Brain and Aging* (New York: Anchor/Doubleday, 1981) provides a sound foundation for understanding Alzheimer's disease (true senile dementia) and the pseudodementias. Henig's final chapter of advice to the middle-aged and to older healthy adults on maintenance of alertness and orientation to reality is useful.

**Your Brain Is Younger Than You Think: A Guide to Mental Aging.** Richard M. Torack. Chicago: Nelson-Hall, 1981. 164p. $14.95; Paper $7.95.

Readable, well-documented, Dr. Torack's presentation of brain structure and normal aging, of the effects of arteriosclerosis (including strokes and high blood pressure) and of depression provide readers threatened with such problems real insight into their personal situations. Torack advises that "the biggest thing that you can do to prevent mental disease is to seek a favorable [stress-free] living environment." He advocates not only research but also a change in popular attitudes toward the elderly.

**The Methuselah Factors: Living Long and Living Well.** Dan Georgakas. New York: Simon & Schuster, 1981. 347p. $14.95.

Based on his investigation of the lives of centenarians, the author concludes that such factors as low caloric intake, regular daily routine, and avoidance of stress are key factors to extended life. No fad diets or easy solutions. A psychological climate in which old age is considered desirable and respected is an important factor in longevity.

**Prolongevity: A Report on the Scientific Discoveries Now Being Made about Aging and Dying, and Their Promise of an Extended Human Life Span—without Old Age.** Albert Rosenfeld. New York: Knopf/Random House, 1976. 250p. $11.95.

Accepting the theory that aging is a genetically regulated process, researchers are exploring means of controlling or reversing bodily decline to achieve a healthy longevity. Personal speculations on the future of true longevity (to over 350 years of age) and the social impacts such a change in life-span would precipitate.

RD 10013

Two accounts of long-lived people may be of interest in connection with these speculations: Grace Halsell's *Los Viejos* (Emmaus, Pa.: Rodale, 1976) and Sula Benet's *How to Live to Be 100: The Life Style of the People of the Caucasus* (New York: Dial Press, 1976). A quite different angle is explored by Osborn Segerberg in *The Immortality Factor* (New York: Dutton, 1974) as he details theories of immortality and ties them to what we know of disease and aging. Witty, sophisticated style over a sound scholarly base; explores the social impacts of earthbound immortality. Saul Kent's *The Life-Extension Revolution* (New York: William Morrow, 1980) explores transplants, cryonics, cloning, and other "breakthroughs" for extended lifespan. For those intellectually curious about possibilities.

## Creative Literature

**"An Old Man."** Guy de Maupassant. In his *Selected Short Stories*, pp. 131-36. New York: Penguin Books, 1971. 368p.

Healthy and active, Monsieur Daron, 86, takes "infinite pains to conceal his age" and is extremely interested in the health and activities of other old people. He keeps track of the health of the ten other town residents over 80 and is relieved when their deaths are "their fault." His philosophy is that those over 80 usually live to 100 because they are the strongest and most sensible of people.

**The Methuselah Enzyme.** Fred M. Stewart. New York: Arbor House, 1970. 244p. $5.95.

A thriller about a rejuvenation treatment in a Swiss youth clinic, *The Methuselah Enzyme* raises crucial personal, social, and political issues relating to endless life for selected humans. With the enzyme "mentase" the biological clock can be turned back, diseases of aging can be cured, and a person can live forever. But the enzyme must be taken from young donors—and that is the problem. A good discussion starter on rejuvenation techniques and medical ethics.
TB 03485

**After Many a Summer Dies the Swan.** Aldous Huxley. New York: Harper & Row, 1965. 246p.

Jo Stoyte, an eccentric and wealthy American in his eighties, hires a British scholar, Jeremy Pordage, to catalog rare diaries from the early 1830s. Their story of the fifth Earl of Gonister, who eats carp intestines to live forever, parallels Stoyte's quest for eternal life. His personal physician, Sigmund Obispo, gives him testosterone treatments and experiments with 200-year-old carp. After reading the Earl's journals, Obispo and Stoyte search for (and find) the Earl alive in his cellar.

RC 12182

**"Dr. Heidegger's Experiment."** Nathaniel Hawthorne.

Old Dr. Heidegger invites four friends to assist him in an experiment with water from the "fountain of youth" in Florida. He observes as they drink the water and are immediately rejuvenated, physically and emotionally. But the results are short-lived and they resume the bodies and personalities of old people. "The water of youth possessed merely a virtue more transient than that of wine.... " This classic tale raises the question of illusion vs. truth as it examines the question of regaining youth. Available in numerous anthologies.

Film. Encyclopaedia Britannica, 1969.

# MAINTAINING HEALTH: DIET AND EXERCISE

**Old Enough to Feel Better: A Medical Guide for Seniors.** Michael Gordon. Radnor, Pa.: Chilton Book Co., 1981. 364p. $14.95.

Dr. Gordon does not assume that increasing age means ill health. Advice for informed health service consumers, with detailed attention to normal diet and special diets related to specific diseases. Includes a brief discussion (pp. 85-93) of sexual expression in later years, an orientation to drugs and their use, and describes a wide range of diagnostic tests. Advice on choice of doctors, preparation for an operation, and on the need for podiatrists and ophthalmologists. A chapter on "common complaints" approaches the discussion from such symptoms as fever, weakness, loss of weight or appetite, etc. Detailed guidance to the layperson on the diseases, treatment, and prognosis for each of the major biological systems (heart, vascular, gastrointestinal, and so forth). A sound, detailed manual written in comfortable prose.

**A Time to Enjoy: The Pleasures of Aging.** Lillian R. Dangott and Richard A. Kalish. Englewood Cliffs, N.J.: Prentice-Hall, 1978. 182p. $11.95.

In this volume that sees aging as a period of significant human growth, useful discussion is included on diet, stress, biofeedback, and the psychodynamics of health.

**The Best Years Catalogue: Solving Problems and Living Fully.**
Leonard Biegel. New York: G. P. Putnam's Sons, 1978. 256p.
$12.95; Paper $6.95.

Described as the "Benjamin Spock for older adults," this upbeat
guide to resources includes lists of medical facilities.

**Feel Better after 50 Food Book.** Adeline Garner Shell and Kay
Reynolds. New York: Sovereign Books/Simon & Schuster,
1978. 218p. $9.95; Paper. Monarch, 1978; Large Type. Boston:
G. K. Hall, 1979. $13.95.

Based on an experimental workshop for older people, this book is
concerned with diet and nutrition and is adapted to special needs of
older adults. Calorie charts; food preparation for easy-to-chew
menus; food selection and storage tips to preserve nutritive value;
simple recipes for the person moving into cooking for the first time.

**A Diet for Living.** Jean Mayer. New York: McKay, 1975. 293p. $8.95.

Questions with answers based on up-to-date knowledge
concerning nutrition, weight, well-being, medical factors, and
exercise. Includes an eating plan, from market to kitchen. Excellent
for the layman.
RC 10043

A multitude of special diet and special cookbooks exist to guide
people with special problems. Just three as a sample: *Diet for a Happy
Heart* by Jeanne Jones (New York: 101 Productions/Scribner, 1975);
*Low Cholesterol Cookbook: Doctor Approved* by Mildred Skinner
(San Antonio, Tex.: Naylor, 1975); and Emil G. Conason and Ella
Metz's *The Salt-Free Diet Cook Book* (New York: Grosset, 1969).

**Be Alive as Long as You Live.** Laurence J. Frankel and Betty Byrd
Richard. New York: Harper & Row, 1980. 239p. $12.95.

Well-illustrated and well-explained exercise program for older
adults.
RC 16748

**Sixty-Plus and Fit Again: Exercises for Older Men and Women.**
Magda Rosenberg. New York: M. Evans and Co., 1977. 156p.
$6.95; Paper. $3.95; Large Type. Boston: G. K. Hall, 1979.
$6.95.

Step-by-step routines to enable the older person to remain agile
and alert at a high level. For the rank beginner as well as for those in
good condition.
RC 12072

**Exercises for the Elderly.** Robert H. Jamieson. Verplanck, N.Y.: Emerson Books, 1982. 158p. $11.95. Large Type.

Simple, detailed instructions (with photographs and graphics) directed toward older adults, with special chapters on exercise for those with handicaps (wheelchair, paralysis, etc.), the bedridden, the confined. Emphasis on regularity of exercise, on moderation in exercise, and on physician's approval of the particular exercise program. Evolved from Jamieson's experience as a physical fitness specialist in retirement homes and convalescent hospitals.

**Aging and Exercise.** Everett L. Smith and Karl G. Stoedefalke. Hillside, N.J.: Enslow Publishing Co., 1982. $8.95.

Excellent instructions and highly satisfactory illustrations for 72 exercises, each measured for energy costs (metabolic units) and with distinction between slow and fast heart rate. For each exercise relevant activities are listed with comparable measure of energy output (e.g., bed-making, canoeing, etc.). See the general discussion in *Exercise and Aging* by Everett L. Smith and Robert C. Serfuss (Hillside, N.J.: Enslow Publishing Co., 1981).

**Over Forty, Feeling Great, and Looking Good.** George Blanda and Mickey Herskowitz. New York: Simon & Schuster, 1978. 155p. $9.95; Paper 1980. $2.95.

A book of exercise and diet by the man famed for playing professional football well into his forties.

RC 12071

**Therapeutic Dance Movement: Expressive Activities for Older Adults.** Erna Caplow-Lindner. New York: Human Sciences Press, 1979. 283p. $29.95; Paper $12.95.

Discussion of the therapeutic values of dance and movement, as well as providing instruction with illustrations on how to teach or lead older people and the disabled in such forms of activity.

## DISEASES ASSOCIATED WITH AGING

**Aging Patients, A Guide for Their Care.** Mary W. Falconer and others. New York: Springer Publishing Co., 1976. 276p. $10.95.

The emphasis is on the common physical and mental diseases of older people. Intended for all paramedical personnel, this book will serve families and friends as well in providing a better life for an aging patient.

**The Longevity Factor.** Walter McQuade and Ann Aikman. New York: Simon & Schuster, 1979. 302p. $10.95.

While designed for people in their forties and fifties, the health profiling approach to disease prevention will serve as well for those in their sixties and seventies. Causes of death covered include arteriosclerotic heart, stroke, cancer, homicide, hypertension, pneumonia, nephritis, cirrhosis of the liver. Diet control, exercise, stress reduction, and avoiding known risks are focused on as lessening risk.

**So You're Going to Have Surgery.** James Graham and Donald G. Cooley. New York: Hawthorne Books, 1970. 280p. $6.95.

Information and advice on the many aspects of having surgery: selection of a surgeon, costs, insurance, preparation and anesthesia, post-operative care and physical therapy. Concise and straightforward.

BRA 04001

**Let the Patient Decide: A Doctor's Advice to Older Persons.** Louis Shattuck Baer. Philadelphia: Westminster Press, 1978. 156p. $5.95.

How to minimize the chances of ending one's life in a nursing home and how to prevent the medical prolongation of the act of dying.

**When Cancer Strikes: A Book for Patients, Families, and Friends.** John A. MacDonald. Englewood Cliffs, N.J.: Prentice-Hall, 1979. 128p. $10.95; Paper $5.95.

Dr. MacDonald was both a surgeon and a victim of cancer. Here he presents information and shares experience in the hope that the terror and the anguish associated with cancer can be alleviated. The chapters "Living with Cancer" and "Dying with Cancer" are especially valuable for the patient and his family.

**Why Me? What Every Woman Should Know about Breast Cancer to Save Her Life.** Rose Kushner. New York: Holt, Rinehart and Winston, 1981. 288p. $7.95; Paper. New York: New American Library, 1977. $2.50.

A freelance writer with some knowledge of medicine, the author gives a personal account of coping with breast cancer. Doctors' attitudes toward surgery and other methods of treatment are discussed along with historic misconceptions, quackeries. Instruction for self-examination is given and the importance of early detection is stressed.

Physical and psychological factors affecting healing are rationally presented.

**Anatomy of an Illness as Perceived by the Patient: Reflection on Healing and Regeneration.** Norman Cousins. New York: W. W. Norton, 1979. 173p. $9.95; Paper. New York: Bantam Books, 1981. $4.95; Large Type. Boston: G. K. Hall, 1980. $10.95.

The opening and closing chapters capture fully the surge of initiative by Cousins as a very ill patient who perceives the importance of his taking responsibility (cooperatively with his physician) for his own recovery. Laughter, vitamin C, and the will to live are the keys to recuperation as Cousins experienced it. Deterioration of the connective tissue was halted and reversed under this regime. Cousins deals with the "placebo effect," with the significance of creativity in the "will to live," and with the phenomenon of pain. For reading and for discussion among those facing serious illness.

RC 14030; RD 14030

**First American Hospice: Three Years of Home Care.** Sylvia A. Lack and Robert W. Buckingham, III. New Haven, Conn.: Hospice, Inc., 1978. 281p. $15.75 (Paper Edition).

The objectives, needs, procedures of providing home care for the terminally ill, with a focus on terminal cancer. Extensive detail sufficient to orient a patient or family at a time when choices are to be made. Many other publications on hospice care are included in the bibliography.

**To Live until We Say Good-bye.** Elisabeth Kübler-Ross. Photos by Mal Warshaw. Englewood Cliffs, N.J.: Prentice-Hall, 1978. 160p. $12.95.

Three of Dr. Kübler-Ross's patients come to terms with death from cancer: Beth, a 42-year-old ex-model; Jamie, a 5-year-old girl; and Louise, a 50-year-old social worker. Half the book is focused on alternatives to hospital care for the dying, and Jack, a recovered alcoholic who has an incurable cancer, is described. Dr. Kübler-Ross, a woman of courage, sensitivity, and insight, has made it possible for us to live openly with the dying, who themselves have won peace and contentment. A liberating, compassionate humanism enables us to avoid the agony and exhaustion associated with cancer.

**A Private Battle.** Cornelius and Kathryn Ryan. New York: Simon & Schuster, 1979. 448p.; Large Type. Stamford, Conn.: Ulverscroft, n.d. $9.95.

The author of *The Longest Day* died of cancer. For four years he kept this secret account of his private battle against the disease.

RC 14541

**Recovering from the Heart Attack Experience: Emotional Feelings, Medical Facts.** Elizabeth S. Weiss and Stephan Rubenstein. New York: Macmillan, 1980. 233p. $12.95.

Patient, family, and friends are guided through the post-heart attack phases of recovery: depression, dependency, and readjustment, with specific advice on therapies, sexual activity, exercise, diet, and other aspects of life necessary to avoid further heart damage. Heart physiology, medication, testing and research in progress are presented as well as a heart attack symptoms chart. Practical manual with a wealth of sound counsel.

**How to Recover from a Stroke and Make a Successful Comeback.** Clarence E. Longnecker. Port Washington, N.Y.: Ashley Books, 1977. 156p. $7.95.

Clear, direct advice to patient and family.

**Episode: Report of an Accident Inside My Skull.** Eric Hodgins. New York: Atheneum, 1981. 272p. $6.95; New York: Simon & Schuster, 1971. $2.95.

The author, struck down by a cardiovascular accident (CVA) tells play by play what it is like physically and psychologically. A man who earned his living writing, he describes with particular insight how it is to have to relearn spelling, reading, and writing.

BRA 02068; CB 00549; RC 16432; TB 00549

**The Western Way of Death: Stress, Tension, and Heart Attacks.** Malcolm Carruthers. New York: Pantheon Books, 1974. 142p. $5.95.

A popular approach to understanding the relation between the stressful way of life and the widespread occurrence of heart attacks. Emphasis on need for exercise, diet, psychotherapy.

BRA 14671

## *Creative Literature*

**Dad.** William Wharton. New York: Knopf, 1981. 416p. $12.95;
  Paper. New York: Avon Books, 1982. $3.50.

After a hospitalization for cancer, Jack, 71, becomes a new, vital
person. His wife, Bette, who is recovering from a heart attack, can't
deal with her "new" husband. Slowly it is revealed that Jack has had a
vivid fantasy life which has sustained him for years. His illness
somehow has caused him to temporarily confuse the two worlds he
lives in. In addition to excellent description of Jack's mental states, the
novel describes his physical decline as well.

**"Growing Old."** Matthew Arnold. In *Poetry of the Victorian Period*,
  p. 500. Edited by George B. Woods. Philadelphia: Richard West,
  1977. $30.00.

A dark, despairing view of old age is represented in this poem
which stresses the physical impairments of age. "It is to feel each limb
grow stiffer, each function less exact." This poem evokes good
discussion, especially when paired with an optimistic piece such as
"Beautiful Old Age" by D. H. Lawrence.

**On Golden Pond.** Ernest Thompson. New York: Dodd, Mead and
  Co., 1979. 191p. $7.95; Paper. New York: New American
  Library, 1981. $2.50.

Norman Thayer, 79, and his wife Ethel, 69, are at their summer
home in Maine for the forty-eighth year. According to the author,
Norman is "flirting with senility"; he also has arthritis, palpitations,
gout, etc. He is preoccupied with the idea of death while Ethel is all
energy and enthusiasm. Although the play is primarily about familial
relationships, Norman exemplifies some typical health problems of
older people, which he becomes able to surmount.
  Film. United Artists, 1981.

**The Spectator Bird.** Wallace Stegner. Garden City, N.Y.: Doubleday,
  1976. 240p. $6.95; Paper. Lincoln: University of Nebraska Press,
  1979. $3.50; Large Type. Boston: G. K. Hall, 1977. $10.95.

Joe and Ruth Allston are in their late sixties, as are most of their
friends near them in northern California. Health and physical
problems are a major concern. An excellent description of arthritis
and its effects on Joe are given on pages 156-64, although this
National Book Award novel concentrates on life review.
  BR 03759

**"Neighbor Rosicky."** Willa Cather. In her *Obscure Destinies*, pp. 3-74. New York: Random House, 1974. 229p. $3.95.

Rosicky, who is 65, has a failing heart; his doctor tells him to take it easy. But he wants to be sure his married son and daughter-in-law, of whom he is proud, are happy. He disobeys orders and has a heart attack. The second one, the next day, kills him, but he knows his obligations and concerns are taken care of. Flashbacks to his life in the big cities of London and New York before he moved to Omaha provide a second theme of city vs. country life.

BR 09986

## COPING WITH LOSS
## OF POWERS

**Blindness: What It Is, What It Does, and How to Live with It.** Thomas J. Carroll. Boston: Little, Brown and Co., 1961. 382p. $3.95.

Discusses the particular limitations suffered by those who have had sight and lost it, the personality difficulties and the constructive, nonsentimental approaches to helping.

TB 00711

**The Hearing Loss Handbook.** Richard Rosenthal. New York: St. Martins Press, 1975. 225p. $8.95.

Anatomy of the ear, construction of different types of hearing aids and problems in their use, and measures the hard of hearing may take to alleviate limitations.

BR 04013

**Growing Old in Silence.** Gaylene Becker. Berkeley: University of California Press, 1980. 160p. $10.00.

Using anthropological perspectives in studying a deaf community, Becker presents a richly textured view of people who are deaf—in all stages of life and adjustment. Seen as human beings with a range of personalities, the deaf approach the problems of aging much as do hearing people, although the problems of dependence on others is not extreme since the lifelong deaf have dealt with this problem earlier. Little attention is given to the problem of the aged who have become deaf in advanced years.

**Reprieve, a Memoir.** Agnes de Mille. Garden City, N.Y.: Doubleday & Company, 1981. 288p. $14.95; Large Type. Boston: G. K. Hall, 1982.

Agnes de Mille, choreographer for *Oklahoma* and *Fall River Legend*, was within an hour of opening her long-dreamed-of Heritage Dance Theatre when she had a massive cerebral hemorrhage that paralyzed the right side of her body. This is Agnes de Mille's own account of her struggle back to independence and professional activity, despite major residual limitations. The road back is full of learning which she richly shares with the reader. Coping with fatigue, learning patience and trust, restoring close ties with husband and sister, exploring new perspectives on life—these are the substance of this human record of life lived fully.

**Long Life: What We Know and Are Learning about the Aging Process.** John Langone. Boston: Little, Brown and Co., 1978. 273p. $9.95.

Personalized approach to the facts of aging, physiological and sociological. Topics dealt with include "rejuvenation," "slowing the clock," and "making the best of it." Addressed as much to men as to women. Readable.

**To Your Good Health! A Practical Guide for Older Americans, Their Families, and Friends.** Edited by Robert V. Skeist. Chicago: Chicago Review Press, 1980. 200p. $5.95.

With a foreword by Maggie Kuhn and contributions by such people as Robert Butler, this layperson's overview is up-to-date and useful indeed.

**The Shattered Mind: The Person after Brain Damage.** Howard Gardner. New York: Knopf, 1975. 481p. $15.00; Paper. New York: Random House, 1976. $6.95.

Identifies the major problems associated with brain damage: aphasia, disorders of language, disturbances of memory, problems in reading.

## Creative Literature

**Wings.** Arthur Kopit. New York: Hill and Wang, 1978. 78p. $8.95; Paper $3.95.

Emily Stilson, in her late seventies, is totally isolated due to brain damage resulting from a stroke. She speaks jargonaphasia (like gibberish) so none of the other characters knows how much she can understand. Only Amy, a therapist at the rehabilitation center, is able to get through to her. The play, originally written for National Public Radio, relies heavily on the sounds Emily hears, thinks, and says, as well as visual images as she perceives them. The play ends with another stroke (or perhaps her death) as she is remembering her earlier life as an aviatrix. A powerfully moving work based on a real person's life.

**Perilous Voyage.** Lael Wertenbaker. Boston: Little, Brown and Co., 1975. 262p.

Augusta MacGregor Turnley, 84, has had an accident which paralyzed her body. But her mind is still intact. In chapter 4 (pp. 42-53) she uses Morse code with her eyelids to signal her doctors and relatives that she wishes to die. When they refuse to obey her, she decides to spend her time reviewing the past and deciding whether her current life is superfluous. Augusta had been a psychic and her granddaughter, Celia, claims to have ESP; she is able to understand what Augusta is thinking much of the time. She and a visiting doctor, Rob Martin, use every device and method possible to stay in communication with Augusta until her death.

RC 08953

**Angle of Repose.** Wallace Stegner. New York: Doubleday, 1971. 569p. $10.00; Paper. New York: Fawcett, 1978. $2.95.

The perspective of Lyman Ward, a 58-year-old amputee who is confined to a wheelchair, is presented in this beautiful novel. The last chapter, "The Zodiac Cottage" (pp. 543-69), is especially good for understanding a disabled person's daily life and his self-concept.

BR 14974; RC 15186

**"Limbo."** Hilary Greenville. *Short Story International* 3 (16): 81-84, October 1979.

Everyone has given up on a brain-damaged, institutionalized woman who cannot speak or move. When Ada, the new ward maid speaks to her, she can feel the fog lift. Her strong emotional response to Ada enables her to utter two words: "Ada, stay." This powerful story is written from the perspective of the patient.

# MENTAL HEALTH

**Stress, Sanity, and Survival.** Robert Woolfolk and Frank Richardson. New York: New American Library, 1979. 210p. $2.25.

Many aspects of this volume will be useful in providing general background to the problems of anxiety and the effective use of worry.

**"Depression: A *Psychology Today* Special Report."** Silvano Arieti and others. *Psychology Today* (April, 1979). Entire Issue.

Depression is the most common functional disease of old age today. The authors discuss its causes, its prevalence in women, and today as the "age of depression."

Leonard Cammer's *Up from Depression* (New York: Simon & Schuster, 1969) defines depression, identifies its symptoms, and advises family members on helpful responses. The author, a psychiatrist, believes that depression yields to treatment.

**Looking Ahead: A Woman's Guide to the Problems and Joys of Growing Older.** Lillian E. Troll and Joan and Kenneth Israel. Englewood Cliffs, N.J.: Prentice-Hall, 1977. 216p. $9.95; Paper $4.95.

Chapters 21 and 22 discuss the professional help available from psychiatrists and the importance of "helping each other."

**You Are Not Alone: Understanding and Dealing with Mental Illness: A Guide for Patient, Families, Doctors and Other Professionals.** Clara Claiborne Park and Leon Shapiro. Boston: Little, Brown and Co., 1976. 496p. $17.50; Paper $8.95.

Chapter 13, "When Your Relative Is Old," is directed to family members who need to know the range of mental illnesses and which ones are reversible. Help in dealing with the full range of problems.

**The End of Senility.** Arthur S. Freese. New York: Arbor House, 1978. 178p. $8.95; Large Type. South Yarmouth, Mass.: John Curley & Associates, 1979. $8.95.

Chapters 5 and 6 on mental health, emotional problems, depression and suicide are readable and sensibly written for the layman.

RC 13576

**Love and Will.** Rollo May. New York: W. W. Norton, 1969. 352p. $14.95; Paper. New York: Dell Publishing Co., 1973. $5.95.

May, a noted psychotherapist and author, acknowledges the schizoid nature of our society and puts the opposing forces into a single framework to creatively propose interconnections among these forces that work for mental health.

TB 02265

**A Time to Enjoy: The Pleasures of Aging.** Lillian J. Dangott and Richard A. Kalish. Englewood Cliffs, N.J.: Prentice-Hall, 1978. 182p. $11.95.

This excellent broad survey of the forces in later years includes very helpful sections on stress, biofeedback, and the psychodynamics of health.

RC 13576

# REORIENTING LIFE TO AGING

Both society and individual older adults have the task of reorientation of life to aging. While society is recognizing that being 60 is not all that different from being 59, the individual at 60 is recognizing the small changes that at 65 mount to meaningful changes and that at 85 have mounted to major changes. Just as society is moving toward accepting older adults as a normal part of society, so the individual over 65 finds it useful to recognize that there are differences. Reorienting life to aging with acceptance of the essential differences and minimizing the social distinctions and unnecessary limitations is a major task of "growing older." This is what Paul Tournier calls "positive acceptance."

Because women are three times as likely as men to survive into old age without a spouse, and because to be a woman and to be old represent two "social disabilities" in our ageist, sexist society, there are many manuals designed to help the older woman reorient her life. But the tasks are basically the same for men and women, as Tournier, Tennenbaum, and Huyck make clear in their books. The assumption of all the authors is that being older does not rule out continued vitality, productivity, and enjoyment of life.

Such reorientation is very strenuous. It challenges self-image and often the older person asks, "Is this indeed I?" Refocus on life goals and values may be needed. Further, family and friends, neighbors and community may begin to behave differently toward the aging adult (who may feel no different at all), and the need to respond with humor, balance, and integrity demand a very solid orientation on the part of the older person.

Rehearsal for the acceptance of new roles has been identified as important. While still in the "middle years" phase of life, it is important to get the feel of a leisurely daily schedule as relaxation rather than restlessness; to try out hobbies before they are looked to as a major time-organizer; to test the skills of making friends in new groups before retirement breaks the network of communication with co-workers. Those who have handled career changes and retirement well are readier to adapt to aging; those who found the "empty nest," divorce, or widowhood manageable, although stressful, are readier to adapt to aging. Recall and analysis of earlier crises will provide encouragement in this later transition into old age. Life satisfaction in the aging person may well reflect the degree to which the process of reorientation was successful.

**Successful Aging.** Olga Knopf. New York: Viking Press, 1975. 229p. $8.95; Large Type. Boston: G. K. Hall, 1977.

This excellent guide to the major tasks and everyday concerns of older adults has an especially useful section (chapters 2 through 4) on reorienting life to aging. Addressed directly to older adults by the author, who woke late to the improtance of this reorientation and chose to help others through the critical transition. Knopf is a professional practitioner of geriatrics.

**Learn to Grow Old.** Paul Tournier. New York: Harper & Row, 1972. 256p. $10.95.

A Swiss psychologist, doctor, and author, Tournier discusses aging in a personal way, showing it to be a beginning as well as a conclusion. For him, what he calls "positive acceptance" of aging is key to this phase of life. He deals with retirement; with the role of the older adult in society, the family, and in intergenerational contacts; with the role of learning ("do it yourself," "educate yourself"); with a second career (for diversity in life, for the opportunity for initiative); and with his Christian faith, which he finds sustaining in facing death. Warmly human.

RD 06591

**Nobody Ever Died of Old Age.** Sharon R. Curtin. Boston: Little, Brown and Co., 1973. 228p. $8.95; Paper $4.95; Large Type. Boston: G. K. Hall, 1972.

Based on a personal survey of a variety of life styles adopted by old people in our society, Curtin has written an unsentimental yet touching and poignant picture of the shelving of the old by society. She calls on the old themselves to join forces to establish new and better roles for themselves.

RD 06375

**Over 55 Is Not Illegal: A Resource Book for Active Older People.** Frances Tennenbaum. Boston: Houghton, Mifflin, 1979. 191p. $14.95; Paper $7.95.

Builds a picture of the new role of older adults in society primarily through the advocating of a battle against ageism, education in the retirement years, voluntarism, participation in community programs, and control of diet and exercise. All this in the context of acceptance of oneself as indeed aging and allied with those who are also older adults.

**The Old Speak Out.** Bonnie Bluh. New York: Horizon Press, 1979. 219p. $10.95.

Based on interviews with over 500 older adults, the book provides personal insights into aging. Each chapter has comments from 6 to 10 persons on a wide variety of topics, including aging. Excellent to start a group discussion.

**Growing Older: The Things You Need to Know about Aging.** Margaret Hellie Huyck. Englewood Cliffs, N.J.: Prentice-Hall, 1974. 179p.

Writing for and to the middle-aged and the young-old adult, Huyck provides a base for positive acceptance of aging in her discussion of the changes and problems and opportunities of the later phase of life (leisure, sexuality, health, death).

BRA 14133; RC 09137

**To the Good Long Life: What We Know about Growing Old.** Morton Puner. New York: Universe Books, 1974. 320p.

An overview of aging as a natural biological event, with social and psychological effects. Informal style for this sound, well-informed book. Includes an interesting summation of theories on *why* we grow old (chapter 4), sound discussions of leisure, sex and marriage, dying, and a fascinating collection of quotations from wise older people on the subject of aging.

BRA 15701

**Aging Is a Family Affair.** Victoria E. Bumagin and Kathryn F. Hirn. New York: Thomas Crowell, 1979. 276p. $10.95.

An anecdotal but extremely well organized, readable introduction to the social, economic, physical, and psychological changes of age. Addressed to the older adult and to the family who share in responsibilities for the older adult.

**More Than Mere Survival: Conversations with Women Over 65.** Jane Seskin. New York: Newsweek Books, 1980. 269p. $8.95.

The versatility of later life is shown through interviews with 22 women, some prominent, some simply from the mass of working people, but all serving as realistic models of independence and self-recognition.

**Going Like Sixty: A Lighthearted Look at the Later Years.** Richard Armour. New York: McGraw-Hill Book Company, 1976. 133p. $3.95.

Armour's humor and light-heartedness, in verse, prose, or drawings, contains a positive and optimistic orientation to aging. Factually sound and realistic in its overview of the aging experience.
    RD 07441

**Mazel Tov! You're Middle-aged.** Albert Vorspan. Garden City, N.Y.: Doubleday, 1974. 128p.

Humorous, witty commentary on middle age leading into old age. Deals with related problems with a warm Jewish accent! Considered are awareness of middle age, mental and physical health, sex life, politics, religion, entertainment, and social concerns.

**Coping: A Survival Manual for Women Alone.** Martha Yates. Englewood Cliffs, N.J.: Prentice-Hall, 1976. 272p. $9.95; Paper $5.95.

A no-nonsense approach from a woman with experience in being alone.

**Being Seventy: The Measure of a Year.** Elizabeth Gray Vining. New York: Viking Press, 1978. 194p.; Large Type. Boston: G. K. Hall, 1978. 289p. $12.95.

This active professional woman completes a book, travels to Japan as an honored guest of the emperor (whom she had tutored when he was Crown Prince), attends a writers' colony for a few weeks, visits with friends, attends committee meetings, and reflects on age, on generational differences, on loneliness and its remedies. "Life is a trust ... to use well, to enjoy, and to give back when the time comes."

**Call It Zest: The Vital Ingredient after Seventy.** Elizabeth Yates. Brattleboro, Vt.: Stephen Greene Press, 1977. 176p. $7.95.

Conversations with eight men and nine women offer profiles of widely different individuals (teacher, writer, physician, minister, diplomat). Focuses on their own aging, their memories, their perspectives on growing older. Yates found the common characteristic elusive, but called it *zest*.

# REHEARSAL FOR AGING: THE MIDDLE YEARS

**Passages: The Predictable Crises of Adult Life.** Gail Sheehy. New York: Dutton, 1976. 393p.; Paper. New York: Bantam Books, 1977. $3.95.

Identifies the crises of life from the twenties through the fifties, drawing on a wealth of illustrations at each stage of adult life. The adult will read with both a sense of recognition and of discovery in these lives of the pacesetter group of motivated middle class men and women.

RD 09919

**The Wonderful Crisis of Middle Age: Some Personal Reflections.** Eda J. LeShan. New York: David MacKay Company, 1973. 339p.; Paper. New York: Warner Books, 1974. $2.95.

Middle age here is 45 to 60 years of age; the problems and issues so empathetically discussed resemble those of aging primarily for their role as rehearsal for the capacity to accept change, new roles, and a new identity. Premonitions that life is not forever, that to be bearable old age must be filled with purpose, concern for others, and interesting activities—these are pieces of rehearsal for aging.

**Hitting our Stride: Good News about Women in Their Middle Years.** Joan Z. Cohen and others. New York: Delacorte Press Books, 1980. 208p.

Joan Cohan and her colleagues, through a widespread questionnaire survey and over 200 interviews, found women in their middle years (35 to 55) feeling more competent than in early life and aware that our society prepares people for young adulthood but not for middle or later years. "We were not raised to be over forty." After mid-life crisis comes a sense of "renewal," with an increased sense of self-awareness, the perception that "we aren't going to live forever," and that facing change is essential. There is the view that each life crisis is rehearsal for the next transition, and that at each "passage" there is opportunity for new beginnings. Excellent section on women's relationships with their husbands, other men, younger men, and on woman-to-woman friendships.

**Gift from the Sea.** Anne Morrow Lindbergh. New York: Random House/Pantheon Books, 1955. 127p. $1.65; Large Type. New York: Franklin Watts, 1955. 128p.

Sensitive and perceptive reflections on the mid-life marriage relationship. The prose flows with poetic beauty and the values illuminate life for the middle-class woman who seeks to restore and hold the beauty of early love. This kind of reflective reassessment (comparable to Florida Scott-Maxwell's *Measure of My Days* at the age of 80) is rehearsal for the life reassessment needed at each stage of the maturing process.

BR 00018; RC 10428

**Single after Fifty: How to Have the Time of Your Life.** Adeline McConnell and Beverly Anderson. New York: McGraw-Hill, 1978. 290p. $9.95; Paper 1980. $3.95.

Written from extensive experience in divorce seminars and Parents without Partners rap sessions, this presentation focuses on problems, concepts and alternatives for both men and women, victims of divorce or widowhood, who have been catapulted into singlehood. Grief stages, rebuilding the new self, establishing the new network of friends and activities, deciding on remarriage, and some recipes for the single chef. The final focus point is that "it's ok to be single; it's ok to be older."

# TASKS
# OF
# MAJOR CHANGE

Changes that threaten our way of life are brought about by many of the events common in later years: retirement, death of those close to us, serious illness, even the way our own aging is reacted to by others. While such events may be foreseen, their impact on our lives is direct and makes heavy demands on our capacity to adjust. When such events cluster in later years, the impact is often severe enough to threaten the sense of continuity of life. Loss of spouse, job, and health within a year or two can shake the orientation of the most sturdy.

Understanding the impact of such losses as part of life experience in later years is necessary on the part of family, friends, and community as well as on the part of the individuals as they suffer these losses. *Role loss* (change of status, loss of loving or effective relationships with others) threatens the sense of personhood and self-esteem. The *social isolation* experienced as one human network breaks down before another builds to replace it can bring the experience of loneliness to an intensity of depression. *Widowhood*, death in the family, and facing one's own death are universally perceived as basic traumas. The study of *death* and of *grief* have brought much insight into our own experiencing of these events and into our capacity to help others in such suffering. We are coming now to recognize that the stages of grief a person goes through on the death of a loved one are applicable in a wide range of human losses (loss through divorce, retirement, departure of adult children from the home, and so forth). Not only are these matters the subjects of helpful learning workshops in church, community agency, or academic environments, but also books and films for the layperson have been skillfully developed to be of significant help. A number of these have been selected for this bibliography.

# ROLE LOSS AND SOCIAL ISOLATION

Social roles, important to the individual throughout life as one means of defining acceptable behavior and of determining self-image, are dependent upon social situation. There are many roles that an individual may fill at any one time: daughter/son, sister/brother, wife/husband, mother/father, neighbor, friend, student, co-worker, boss, volunteer, and so forth. Middle age is notable for the number of roles an individual fills simultaneously.

As the individual enters old age, however, the number of roles he fills may decrease sharply. With retirement, with the death of siblings, parents, or spouse, with ill health cutting activity in neighborhood and community, the number of roles is severely diminished. Loss of status, prestige, and financial security may accompany these role losses. Many of these role losses, unlike those in middle years, are not a matter of choice but are imposed by societal decree or natural events over which the individual has no control. While there are some useful books interpreting this experience from the nonfiction context, more direct understanding may come from the reading of creative literature.

**Aging: An Album of People Growing Old.** Shura Saul. New York: John Wiley, 1974. 192p. $10.95.

Fine photographs and sensitive text depict human beings in the dilemmas of aging. Pages 13 to 19 depict "The World of the Aging Person."

**Old Folks at Home.** Alvin Rabushka and Bruce Jacobs. New York: Free Press, 1980. 202p. $10.95.

Depicting older adults as homeowners with moderate incomes, the authors nevertheless see older adults as a segregated and increasingly dependent group. The authors propose a restructuring of federal programs, increased reliance on local support, and enhanced independence of the aged.

**Leavetaking: When and How to Say Goodbye.** Mortimer R. Feinberg and others. New York: Simon & Schuster, 1978. 286p.

The pattern of role change, severance of linkage in familiar networks, is here generalized to apply to death, divorce, separation of unmarried couples, job loss, retirement, loss of elderly parents, and the empty nest. Techniques and strategies for leavetaking are the focus of the book.

**Recovering: A Journal.** May Sarton. New York: W. W. Norton, 1980. 246p. $12.95; Large Type. Boston: G. K. Hall, 1981.

For May Sarton her sixty-sixth year was a time of personal loss in friendship, in love, in health, in status as a writer. This is a sensitively reported account of her moving through deep depression and putting her life in focus again.

**Aging: The Fulfillment of Life.** Henri J. M. Nouwen and Walter J. Gaffney. Garden City, N.Y.: Doubleday, 1974. 160p. $2.95.

Nouwen and Gaffney, in a book with beautiful photographs to underscore the message of the text, depict first the loss of self that comes with physical change, social segregation, and the desolation from broken contacts with both the living and the dead. The rewards of aging in the fulfillment of the meaning of life is the counterpart of their text, and the photographs fully reflect the caring, joyful, or intellectually perceptive older adults for whom more years have added richness. Caring, compassion, and a prizing of life for each person are themes of this warmly human understanding of life within a broadly religious context.

**In the Fullness of Time.** Avis D. Carlson. South Bend, Ind.: Henry Rognery, 1977. 195p.; Large Type. South Yarmouth, Mass.: John Curley & Associates, 1979. $10.95.

Aware that "somebody needs to write from the inside about the experience of aging," Carlson at the age of 80 pulled together basic facts and set them in the framework of her own experiences and those of friends and acquaintances. "Somebody should be pointing out how hard it is to maintain a feeling of self-worth." Wise, sound counsel and a mature perspective on aging.

RD 11801

**Life's Second Half: The Pleasures of Aging.** Jerome Ellison. Old Greenwich, Conn.: Devin-Adair, 1978. 172p. $8.95; Large Type. Boston: G. K. Hall, 1979. $13.95.

Ellison is the founder of the Phoenix Society, a nationwide affinity group for older citizens with an "up" philosophy for the aging. The book, however, offers practical and empathetic solutions to the severe problems facing older persons: abrupt, involuntary retirement, widowhood, etc., shaping what the author calls a "new gerontology."
BR 03991; RD 13204

**Vintage: The Bold Survivors!** Joan Dufault. New York: Pilgrim Press, 1978. 256p. $12.95.
Life perspectives in profusion, drawing seasoned commentary from those rich in years and living, from across the world: Dorothy Brett, English painter and living her last years in Taos; Jim Bell, Alabama farmer; John James Haran, a New York Irish-American bartender; a not-yet-retired British professor of 80 living in Oxford; a lemon vendor in Nice, France ... 38 in all. Superb photographs and excellently edited retrospective comments (each on his or her own life experience), together with brief introductions by the editor-photographer of how she came to talk with each person. Here are people who have lived through many role changes to achieve the fullness of self-realization.
RD 13938

**Looking Ahead: A Woman's Guide to the Problems and Joys of Growing Older.** Lillian E. Troll and Joan and Kenneth Israel. Englewood Cliffs, N.J.: Prentice-Hall, 1977. 216p. $9.95; Paper $3.95.
Realistic appraisal of problems for women who in their youth use beauty as their base for self-image, and those who wield power as the core of their egos, and the dilemmas they face in the older years. Constructive, sound commentary.

**Lonely in America.** Suzanne Gordon. New York: Simon & Schuster, 1976. 318p. $8.95.
Concerned with loneliness of the urban and suburban white middle class, Gordon as journalist interviewed many adults and concluded that divorce, mobility, and loss of a sense of community are at the root of the problem, and that old age is only one of the phases of life for which this is a major anguish.

### Creative Literature—Role Loss

**Celebration.** Harvey Swados. New York: Simon & Schuster, 1974. 348p.; New York: Dell Publishing Co., 1976. $1.95.

*Celebration* is a journal of five months in the life of Samuel Lumen, a famous educator. He starts the diary "to ease the stupid burden of being old" a few months before his ninetieth birthday, which is to be celebrated by a television special and a White House party. This occasion heightens the struggle between his public and private lives, between those who treat him as a living monument and those who still expect him to change.

RD 08183

**Storm Weather.** August Strindberg. In *The Chamber Plays of August Strindberg*, pp. 3-53. Minneapolis: University of Minnesota Press, 1981. $6.95.

The old gentleman, a retired civil servant in his mid-sixties, has lived in his apartment, "the quiet house," for 10 years, and is "content with old age and its quiet peace." Greda, his ex-wife, disrupts his orderly life when she returns for help in finding her new husband and their child. When all is settled he looks forward to moving out of that apartment and returning to a serene life.

**Mr. Sammler's Planet.** Saul Bellow. New York: Viking Press, 1970. 313p. $8.95; New York: Penguin Books, 1977. $2.50.

Artur Sammler, a 70-year-old concentration camp survivor, lives in New York City with his daughter, Shula, and his niece, Margotte. His experiences in the bustling city demonstrate to him his change of status. In one scene, he witnesses a pickpocketing: "He was old.... He knew what to do, but had no power to execute it." A feeling of helplessness and dismay permeate his life and this novel.

BR 04414; TB 03110

**Death of a Salesman.** Arthur Miller. New York: Viking Press, 1949. 139p. $10.00; New York: Penguin Books, 1976. $2.25.

In this dramatic play, Willy Loman re-examines his relationship with his sons and his self-concept after being forced to retire as a traveling salesman. Unable to deal with his new status and lifestyle, Willy commits suicide. This penetrating and thought-provoking play is often performed locally.

BR 02719; TB 102609; Film. Columbia, 1951.

**Poorhouse Fair.** John Updike. New York: Knopf, 1977. 185p. $9.95; New York: Fawcett Book Group, 1981. $2.50.

John F. Hook, 94, is a retired school teacher. He lives in a home for the poor elderly in New Jersey, run by a well-meaning man, Mr.

Conner. The novel centers around the annual fair given at the poorhouse and on the relationships between the residents. But a strong theme is the loss of status for Mr. Hook, who still considers himself a learned and wise man without a class to teach.

BR 01995

**The Oldest Living Graduate.** Preston Jones. In his *A Texas Trilogy*, pp. 235-338. New York: Hill and Wang, 1976. 338p. $8.95.

This two-act play is the last of a trilogy about Bradleyville, Texas, a town of 6,000. Colonel J. C. Kincaid, 75, is a wheelchair-bound stroke victim who lives there with his son, Floyd. The Mirabeau B. Lamar Military Academy decides to honor its oldest living graduate, the Colonel, at the dedication of its new school. The Colonel is used as an object by the school, for its ceremony, and by his son, for his land. He deeply resents the loss of respect and position he once enjoyed. "It ain't no honor being the oldest living *anything*. Oldest living *graduate*, oldest living *Indian*, oldest living *armadillo*, oldest living *nuthin'*, 'cause that means that you're all alone!"

**A Late Encounter with the Enemy.** Flannery O'Connor. In her *Complete Stories*, pp. 134-44. New York: Farrar, Straus, and Giroux, 1979. 555p. $20.00; Paper $8.95.

General Sash, 104, is to be the star attraction at his granddaughter's graduation. The thought of him on the platform in his Civil War uniform means a lot to her, Sally Poker Sash, age 62. His life is boring except for the annual Confederate Memorial Day festivities when he is displayed as a relic. He dies on the stage during the ceremony and nobody notices.

RC 15019

**Mrs. Stevens Hears the Mermaids Singing.** May Sarton. New York: W. W. Norton, 1974. 240p. $6.95; Paper 1975. $3.95.

Hilary Stevens, a 70-year-old poet of renown, is to be interviewed about her life and career. This novel deals with her self-definition and self-pride as an artist and as an older person. "I earned being old.... Don't deprive me of what I earned." Portrayal of a strong, independent, proud woman.

**Memento Mori.** Muriel Spark. New York: Time, 1964. 246p.

Charmian Colston, 85, is a popular novelist, with many friends and acquaintances, but has a poor memory. Her husband, Godfrey, 87, is envious of her fame and threatens to institutionalize her.

Charmian and Godfrey, as well as his sister Lettie, and various friends, live in their own homes. Miss Taylor, Charmian's retired servant, and another group of people live in a nursing home in town. Spark's thesis appears to be that in old age people remain whatever they were before, neither more fair nor more mean, neither more wise nor more petty. Neither age nor wealth alters a person's personality. Excellent topic for a heated discussion.

TB 02953

## Creative Literature — Social Isolation

**The Gin Game.** D. L. Coburn. New York: Drama Books Specialists, 1978. 73p. $7.95.

Fonsia Dorsey and Weller Martin live at the Bentley Nursing and Convalescent Home where they play gin rummy on the sun porch. Each has a family who doesn't visit; each is too proud to admit loneliness. This Pulitzer Prize-winning play takes place during two weeks on the porch.

BR 04244; RD 14023

**As We Are Now.** May Sarton. New York: W. W. Norton, 1973. 136p. $10.95.

Caro Spencer, 76, starts a journal, "The Book of the Dead," in order to keep her sanity while in a nursing home. She describes its purposes beautifully on page 10. And on page 14 she refers to her life as solitary confinement. "Whatever I have now is my own mind." Moving and realistic except for the ending. Good as a basis for discussion.

RD 07015

**"Miss Brill."** Katherine Mansfield. In *Collected Stories*, pp. 330-35. London: Constable, 1968.

Miss Brill goes to the park each Sunday afternoon to escape "her room like a cupboard." She enjoys the band concerts and the people in the audience. But this time an unfeeling, insulting comment by a young couple spoils her weekend ritual.

There's a happier ending to "The Key" by Isaac Bashevis Singer (*Short Story International*, 3(12):139-50, February, 1979). Bessie Popkin, alone in New York after her husband has died, breaks her doorkey in the lock and discovers that she has some good neighbors, and that her daily life need not be one of despair and loneliness.

**"Agatha."** John O'Hara. In his *The Hat on the Bed*, pp. 3-16. New York: Random House, 1962. 405p.

Agatha Child is a rich heiress in her mid-fifties who has survived the last of her three husbands and now lives alone with her two dogs. She lives a lonely, pretentious, and empty life centered on obtaining full-time help, buying new clothes, and thinking about the past.

Another lonely woman, dependent on hired help for companionship, is Miss Briggs in "Little Dog" by Langston Hughes. (In his *The Ways of White Folks*, pp. 156-70. New York: Knopf, 1934; New York: Random House, 1971.) Miss Briggs is increasingly lonely after the death of her mother. When she realizes how much she looks forward to seeing the friendly black waiters and janitor, she moves away. A sad, thought-provoking story.

**"The Trinket Box."** Doris Lessing. In her *African Stories*, pp. 26-39. New York: Popular Library, 1975. 670p. $2.95.

Ageless, energetic, unmarried Aunt Maud has always been an unpaid servant to her relatives, moving wherever her help was needed with a new baby, sick child, or whatever. She has also traveled as the companion to needy friends. Although she was always the perfect guest, sending gifts and cards, her relatives felt irritation toward her rather than gratitude. A portrait of an unloved, lonely, proud woman.

**"Heartache."** Anton Chekhov. In *We Are but a Moment's Sunlight*, pp. 174-80. Edited by Charles S. Adler. New York: Pocket Books, 1976. 252p. $1.95.

Iona Potapov, a widower, lives a lonely life with only other cabbies and his fares to talk with. When his son dies, none of them listens to his sorrow; Iona has only his horse to talk to.

**"The Death of the Hired Man."** Robert Frost.

Frost's narrative poem is most famous for its line "Home is the place where, when you have to go there,/they have to take you in." Although Silas has a wealthy brother, he does not feel as at home there as at Mary and Warren's farm. Silas, an old hired hand, returns there, offering to work for them again. Although Warren feels that Silas is useless to them, he and Mary agree to accept him. Warren goes to talk with him only to find that Silas has died "at home" with them.

**"Leaving the Yellow House."** Saul Bellow. In his *Mosby's Memoirs and Other Stories*, pp. 3-42. New York: Viking Press, 1968. 184p. $6.95; Paper. New York: Penguin Books, 1977. $1.95.

Living alone in the yellow house at Sego Desert, Hattie, 72, drinks a lot and smokes a lot. When she has a car accident, she never recovers from her broken arm, and realizes that she can no longer live alone. She begins to worry about the house, which was willed to her by a former employer 20 years before. Worry about the house becomes central to her life. "In addition to everything else, why must I worry about this, which I must leave? I am tormented out of my mind ... cast off and lonely." The story ends with her postponing—yet again—a decision about her future and the house's.

RC 10874; TB 03009

**Good Morning, Midnight.** Jean Rhys. New York: Random House, 1974. 159p. $2.95.

A friend rescues Sasha Jansen from despair and drink by sending her on a trip to Paris, where she had once lived. But the memories in Paris only accentuate her loneliness and isolation; her impulse is to remain in the past and avoid any consideration of her future. "What do I care about anything when I can lie on the bed and pull the past over me like a blanket?"

**"A Stroke of Luck."** In *Solo: Women on Women Alone*, pp. 152-60. Edited by Linda and Leo Hamalian. New York: Dell Publishing Co., 1977. 367p. $1.95.

When the grandmother has a stroke at 73, she feels that she will finally receive the attention and love from her family that she has so sorely missed. A powerful tale of loneliness and isolation in a stingy, uncaring family. The title refers to the daughter's comment that it was a "stroke of luck" that the grandmother had such a lovely, sunny hospital room; it also refers to the protagonist's reaction to her illness, and to the readers' response to her death.

**"Where the Cloud Breaks."** H. E. Bates. In *The Best of H. E. Bates*, pp. 414-25. Boston: Little, Brown and Co., 1963. 454p.

Colonel Gracie is proud of not having a telephone. When he wants to speak with his friend and neighbor, Miss Wilkinson, he runs up a signal flag. Since he has taught her how to use them, she can respond. He also has no calendar or clock; he can rely on her to know the date and time. But when she receives a television set, he ends their friendship. Both characters in this excellent story are old and alone, lonely and isolated. But the Colonel's pride in his isolation keeps them apart.

**"The Old Woman and Her Cat."** Doris Lessing. In *Solo: Women on Women Alone*, pp. 332-48. Edited by Leo and Linda Hamilian. New York: Dell Publishing Co., 1977. 367p. $1.95.

Hetty, an older woman, has lived alone since the death of her husband and the desertion of her children. She has become an eccentric beggar, a "shopping bag lady," with only her pets to cherish. When she is to be evicted from her flat for keeping a cat, to avoid being put into an institution, she moves into an abandoned building where she dies of exposure. Excellent storytelling.

**"Madame Zilensky and the King of Finland."** Carson McCullers. In her *The Ballad of the Sad Cafe and Other Stories*, pp. 103-112. New York: Bantam Books, 1967. $2.50.

Madame Zilensky, an old woman who is a renowned musician, seems to be a pathological liar to the dean of the music department where she now works. Slowly he comes to realize that her life has been totally devoted to her music, and that she lives vicariously in her fantasies.

BR 01092

**"What Do You Hear from 'Em?"** Peter Taylor. In *Stories of the Modern South*, pp. 343-58. Edited by Ben Forkner and Patrick Samway. New York: Bantam Books, 1977; New York: Penguin Books, 1981. $4.95.

Ageless Aunt Munsie waits for her annual visit from Will and Thad, her employer's sons, and for their return to Thornton. Finally she realizes that they will never move back there and that time will not turn backward for her. A strong portrayal of a lonely, isolated old woman.

TB 02964

**"The Geologist's Maid."** Anne Tyler. In *Stories of the Modern South*, pp. 359-70. Edited by Ben Forkner and Patrick Samway. New York: Bantam Books, 1977; New York: Penguin Books, 1981. $4.95.

Dr. Bennett Johnson, a sick, white elderly geologist, and Maroon, his black elderly maid, are completely dependent on each other. Yet they live in two totally separate worlds in Baltimore, Maryland.

# WIDOWHOOD

For most married people the death of a spouse is the most severe trauma. The basic human need for intimacy has typically been structured in the context of marriage. One's roots, continuity, and identity are centered here. One's social life is built around couplehood; others relate to each of the couple as married. Status of women currently 60 years or older has clearly been tied to the marriage. The daily, weekly, seasonal patterns of living tend to have been tied to the married state. A break in the married life for the older man or woman involves the physical, emotional, and mental health and resources of the surviving spouse.

Because of its powerful impact, widowhood has been extensively studied, and help in books is abundantly available — for understanding in advance of the death (or later) and for solace and support.

**Widow.** Lynn Caine. New York: Bantam Books, 1975. 192p. $2.25.

The author's account of her husband's death while they were in middle years and of her long struggle back to self-confidence carries many honest statements of her suffering and concern, shared inevitably by older women when widowed. While the sexual and companionship adjustments in age may be somewhat different, the crux of the problem is the same: How to become a separate self after years of marriage. Tough, lucid, tactful, skillful writing. A basic book on widowhood. Good for discussion among older women.

BRA 15517; RD 07512

**The Widower.** Jane Burgess Kohn and Willard K. Kohn. Boston: Beacon Press, 1978. 169p.; Paper 1979. $4.95.

Written for men at the period of immediate personal loss. Although not related solely to the older marriage loss, the sound and sympathetic perceptions provide an important personal/professional viewpoint on the situation of the older adult. Women as well as men will be interested in this for reading and discussion.

RD 11213

**Helping Each Other in Widowhood.** Edited by Phyllis R. Silverman and others. New York: Health Sciences Publishing Corporation, 1974. 212p. $8.95.

How the Widow-to-Widow program works structurally, and — even more significantly — reports from some of the Widow-to-Widow chapters, plus detailed advice on "how to help." The role of volunteers and their training, the role of professional people in the basically volunteer program. A final helpful section on "death, grief, and bereavement."

**But I Never Thought He'd Die: Practical Help for Widows.** Miriam Baker Nye. Philadelphia: Westminster Press, 1978. 150p. $4.95.

A guide for widows to facing facts, understanding feelings, identifying and carrying out developmental tasks and setting new goals.

**Love Must Not Be Wasted: When Sorrow Comes, Take It Gently by the Hand.** Isabella Taves. Scranton, Pa.: Thomas Y. Crowell Co., 1974. 214p.

A widow recounts her experience in facing the terminal illness of her husband (with its inevitable questions of relationship in the final period of dying), and compares her experience with the experiences of her friends facing similar situations. Then the weeks and months of grieving, adjustments, re-emergence and the recognition of her own power to love and acceptance of that even in single widowhood.

BRA 13281; RD 07581

**A Widow's Pilgrimage.** Jean Hersey. New York: Seabury Press, 1979. 114p. $7.95.

A personal account of loss of a close and dear husband after 50 years of marriage. In diary format Jean Hersey records the stages of her grief from the initial shock and disbelief, to "giving up on life," to final acceptance of Robert's death and her new responsibilities and a new way of life. The brevity and warmth of this book lends itself to group sharing of insights in literature discussion or in group therapy. The recently widowed will find comfort and inspiration here.

**Merry Widow.** Grace Nies Fletcher. New York: William Morrow, 1970. 255p.

Cheerful autobiographical reminiscences that cover the period of her childhood, marriage, and children in the context of her loss of her husband. Shows a wholesome evolution from widow to "merry widow" over a decade, bringing her back to appreciation of life and laughter and adventure. Implicit encouragement to widows to build a new life and enjoy enjoyment!

BRA 00763

**Looking Ahead: A Woman's Guide to the Problems and Joys of Growing Older.** Lillian E. Troll and Joan and Kenneth Israel. Englewood Cliffs, N.J.: Prentice-Hall, 1977. 216p. $9.95; Paper $3.95.

Among the many excellent approaches to aging for women, chapter 9 is devoted to the meaning of friendship in widowhood.

**Leavetaking: When and How to Say Goodbye.** Mortimer R. Feinberg and others. New York: Simon & Schuster, 1978. 286p.

Leavetaking is seen as a necessary human process, involving painful disruption of personal roles and loss of others. The pattern of grieving in death loss is clearly outlined: shock and disbelief; developing awareness with anguish or anger; restitution and mourning; resolving loss; idealization; remembrance with a degree of objectivity. Anecdotes center as frequently on men's roles as on women's.

RC 12083

**Teach Your Wife How to Be a Widow.** Edited by Joseph Newman. New York: U.S. News and World Report/Simon & Schuster, 1974. 301p.

While the money world has changed since 1974, this clear presentation of mortgages, wills, insurance, investments, health care, and social security remains a useful presentation to any beginner.

## Creative Literature

**"Old Love."** Isaac Bashevis Singer. In his *Passions*, pp. 24-42. New York: Farrar, Straus, Giroux, 1975. 273p. $8.95; Paper. Fawcett Book Group, 1978. $2.95; Large Type. South Yarmouth, Mass.: John Curley & Associates, 1966.

Harry Beudiner, 82, lives alone in Miami Beach in a condominium full of other old people. A widower, he claims to need no housekeeper or wife. But when his new neighbor, Ethel Brokles, introduces herself one afternoon, he decides to marry her and share his life and wealth. That night, Ethel, unbespoke, still mourning her husband, and recovering from a nervous breakdown after his death, commits suicide. Harry, lonelier than ever, is left alone again.

BR 03165; RC 09730

**"A Negative Balance."** April Wells. In *Solo: Women on Women Alone*, pp. 94-100. Edited by Leo and Linda Hamalian. New York: Dell, 1977. $1.95.

A nameless woman, widowed a year, leads a lonely and anxious life. Although she says that she has dealt with her husband's death, it is clear to the reader that she has not begun a new life. An unexpected visit from a 20-year-old, distant relative who is "bumming" it across the country, illuminates her isolation and fears. Barely seven pages long, this story paints an excellent portrait of a lonely older woman.

**The Human Season.** Edward Lewis Wallant. New York: Harcourt, Brace, Jovanovich, 1973. 192p. $1.65.

When Joe Berman, 59, unexpectedly loses his wife, Mary, he's angry and confused. A Russian Jewish immigrant, plumber by trade, he feels unfairly jeopardized by his age, which he considers to be halfway between a stage at which he could begin again and a stage at which he could be "the old grandpa." At first he rejects his daughter's invitation to live with her family but later he accepts it and moves out of his house.

# GRIEF AND GRIEVING

The grieving process is a normal, even necessary, one and occurs many times throughout our lives. Not only do we grieve losses of those dear to us through death but many other kinds of loss as well. The departure of children from the home, the loss involved in moving from one location to another, the loss of a job (for whatever reason), even the loss of a previous self-concept, all may cause grief to those who suffer the losses. For the aging person, multiple losses may occur within a short time, not the least of which includes the loss of spouse, life-long friends, or the loss felt at one's own approaching death. Society's understanding of the stages and manifestations of grieving is essential if support is to be given to those in the grieving process.

Feinberg's *Leavetaking* identifies well-defined stages of grief: shock and disbelief, anguish and anger, mourning, resolving loss, idealization, and ultimately remembrance with objectivity. Research has now shown that grieving is an essential process, and that unresolved grief and grief denial are a destructive force throughout a lifetime. Grieving must be understood.

**Leavetaking: When and How to Say Goodbye.** Mortimer R. Feinberg and others. New York: Simon & Schuster, 1978. 286p.

Leavetaking is seen as a necessary human process, involving painful disruption of personal roles and loss of others. While loss by death is seen as one of the greatest losses, the pattern of grieving in death is paralleled in loss by divorce: shock and disbelief; developing awareness with anguish or anger; restitution and mourning; resolving loss; idealization; remembrance with a degree of objectivity. Case examples are abundant, including death, divorce, separation of unmarried couples, job loss, loss of elderly parents, and "empty nest." Anecdotes center as frequently on men's roles as on women's. Techniques and strategies for leavetaking are the focus.

RC 12083

**Understanding Grief.** Edgar N. Jackson. Nashville, Tenn.: Abingdon Press, 1957. 255p. $7.95.

Explores the dynamics of grief, the role of guilt, the function of a religious philosophy in handling the grief experience.

**The Gift of Grief: Healing the Pain of Everyday Losses.** Ira J. Tanner. New York: Hawthorn Books, 1976. 167p.; Minneapolis, Minn.: Winston Press, 1980. 184p. $4.95.

An exploration of the phenomenon of grief and our complex reactions to it. Tanner relates coping with loss to constructive change, and demonstrates the destructive power of unresolved grief and grief denial.

**Bereavement: Studies of Grief in Adult Life.** Colin Murray Parkes. Garden City, N.Y.: International Universities Press, 1972. 233p. $17.50.

Describes the stages of grieving, the process of gaining a new identity, normal and unhealthy bereavement, methods of helping the grieved, and the relationships between loss by death and other types of permanent separation from people and things. Drawn from extensive study of widows and their reactions to loss.

**Living — When a Loved One Has Died.** Earl A. Grollman. Boston: Beacon Press, 1977. 115p. $7.95; Paper $4.95.

How to help one manage wisely the emotions of grief.

RC 11577

**Peace of Mind.** Joshua L. Liebman. New York: Simon & Schuster, 1965. 186p. $2.95; Large Type $8.95; New York: New American Library, 1976. $1.50.

Essays which suggest ways of achieving peace of mind through a correlation of the discoveries of modern dynamic psychology with the truest religious insights and the goals of the ages.

**When Bad Things Happen to Good People.** Harold S. Kushner. New York: Schocken Books, 1981. 160p. $10.95; Paper. New York: Avon Books, 1983. $3.50.

Spurred by his own experience of pain (his first-born son gradually succumbed to progeria, "rapid aging"), Rabbi Kushner tries to make sense out of random wounding and "undeserved" misfortune in a life of faith and goodwill. Many make the same struggle and will find Kushner's reflections supportive.

**A Time to Love, A Time to Die.** Prince Leopold Loewenstein. New York: Doubleday/Pyramid Publications, 1971. 276p.

A sensitive telling of a man's love for his wife who is ill and about to die. Emphasis on how he is able to cope.

RD 06663; TB 03871

Similar tributes by writers to the memory of their deceased wives: C. S. Lewis's *Grief Observed* (New York: Seabury Press, 1961; New York: Bantam Books, 1976) and Alan Paton's *For You, Departed* (New York: Scribner's Sons, 1969. Az-BPH (AZ CB 141) RC; BR 01158).

**The Healing Power of Grief.** Jack Silvey Miller. New York: Seabury Press, 1978. 125p.

A volume of meditations dealing with death that arrives in a multitude of forms—ill health, accident, violence, suicide, deprivation. For each meditation, there is a statement of "in memoriam." For clergy or lay pastors, guidance in working with the bereaved.

**Death's Single Privacy: Grieving and Personal Growth.** Joyce Phipps. New York: Seabury Press, 1974. 143p.

Joyce Phipps recounts her own experiences related to the death of her husband when they were in their middle years. Telling the children, receiving support from friends and neighbors, making death real and seeing life as having a new beginning, being a "woman alone." Protestant religious belief aspects of accepting death.

**A Time to Enjoy: The Pleasures of Aging.** Lillian R. Dangott and Richard A. Kalish. Englewood Cliffs, N.J.: Prentice-Hall, 1978. 182p. $11.95; Paper $4.95.

The brief sections on grief and mourning and on death and dying are excellent introductions to basic understanding of these experiences.

**Aging Is a Family Affair.** Victoria E. Bumagin and Kathryn F. Hirn. New York: Thomas Crowell, 1979. 276p. $10.95.
Especially empathetic to the problems of grief and dying.

**Recovering: A Journal.** May Sarton. New York: W. W. Norton, 1980. 246p. $12.95; Large Type. Boston: G. K. Hall, 1981. $12.95.
May Sarton continues her journal in *Recovering*, showing her personal maturing in recognizing the needed alternatives to possessive love, in accepting the writer's risk of harsh, insensitive public criticism that challenges the ego, in experiencing the grief over loss of a relationship with a close friend who enters senility. She sees death's power to restore our friends to us. She undergoes a mastectomy. These deep human experiences in her sixty-sixth year are the intense human communication in the context of the daily journal, where household animals, the garden, the Maine coast, the multitude of friends and visitors provide the normalizing effect that allows daily joys and healing perspectives.

**Life Is Victorious! How to Grow through Grief.** Diane Kennedy Pike. New York: Simon & Schuster/Pocket Books, 1977. 209p. $1.95.
The author shares her touching and moving experience and details how she came to terms with the death of her husband.

**The Sorrow and the Fury: Overcoming Hurt and Loss from Childhood to Old Age.** Lucy Freeman. Englewood Cliffs, N.J.: Prentice-Hall, 1978. 152p.
The author draws on insights she gleaned from her own analysis and from talking with psychoanalysts and other experts to fully explore the dynamics of loss.

**Anticipatory Grief.** Bernard Schoenberg and others. New York: Columbia University Press, 1974. 336p. $20.00.
These professional papers on "anticipatory grief" focus on the grieving by family, friends, or the dying patient himself in anticipation of losses about to take place. The first five chapters at least are quite useful to the lay counselor or to the educated layman struggling with anticipatory grief. Comparisons between traditional grief and anticipatory grief are usefully made.

**Learning to Say Good-By: When a Parent Dies.** Eda J. LeShan. New York: Macmillan, 1976. 85p. $8.95; New York: Avon Books, 1978. $3.95.

While this book helps adults understand the problems a child faces in the death of a parent, there are implications for preparing a child to understand and accept the death of an older adult (grandparent, etc.) as well. The need for children to participate in mourning, in funerals is made clear.

## Creative Literature

**"Heartache."** Anton Chekhov. In *We Are but a Moment's Sunlight*, pp. 174-80. Edited by Charles S. Adler. New York: Pocket Books, 1976. 252p. $1.95.

Iona Potapov, an elderly widower who drives a cab, mourns the death of his son alone. None of his fares, or fellow cabbies, will listen to him. So he shares his grief with his horse. This is a short, poignant tale of lonely grieving.

**"Old Man Minnick."** Edna Ferber. In *Intimate Relationships: Marraige, Family, and Lifestyles through Literature*, pp. 225-39. Edited by Rose M. Somerville. Englewood Cliffs, N.J.: Prentice-Hall, 1975. 480p. $16.95; Paper $11.95.

When Ma dies at 65, Pa, who's nearly 70, is shocked; he'd assumed he'd die first. Because of financial problems resulting from her medical bills and the stock market crash that year, Pa moves in with his son, George, and his wife, Nettie. Although they are good to him, he mourns his wife and is lonely. "He got kindness, but he needed love." The companionship of other older men, who spend their days at the park, is what finally helps Old Man Minnick to start a new life.

**"Back to Back."** Bruce Jay Friedman. In *Familiar Faces*, pp. 62-86. Edited by Pat McNees. New York: Fawcett Book Group, 1979. $2.25.

Harry Towns, an upper middle-class screenwriter, is mourning the death of his parents "back to back." He feels guilty that he procrastinated in moving them out of their old neighborhood into a nice apartment until it was too late; he feels he had failed in his responsibility to his parents, who were in their seventies. Excellently written, portraying Harry's mourning without sentimentality, this story is excerpted from *About Harry Towns* (New York: Knopf, 1974).

**The Eye of the Storm.** Patrick White. New York: Viking, 1974.
   608p. $8.95; Paper. New York: Avon Books, 1975. $2.50.

   The concluding chapters of this novel depict Elizabeth Hunter's
servants trying to accept her death. Although she had been a
domineering woman, they were fond of her and hate to leave her now-
empty house. The head nurse, Sister de Santis, takes a new assignment
but finds herself thinking only of Elizabeth. Mrs. Kippman, the cook,
commits suicide rather than start in a new employ. Their reactions are
in sharp contrast to those of the middle-aged children, Dorothy and
Basil, who are anxious to return to their own homes and lives.

   RD 07253

**"Pantaloon in Black."** William Faulkner. In his *Go Down, Moses*,
   pp. 90-108. New York: Random House, 1928; Paper 1973. $2.45.

   Rider, a black sawmill worker, is unable to accept the death of his
wife. As he takes out his grief in violence, he becomes progressively
isolated from his friends and neighbors, and is eventually lynched by
the white town people. A strong story, helped by discussion not only
of the portrayal of grief, but of the racist reactions of the townfolk.

   BR 02086; BR 13870; RD 06216

# DEATH AND DYING

   One of the great social revolutions of our generation is moving
death out of the shadows and into the spotlight. Elisabeth Kübler-
Ross, with her physician's analysis of the psychological stages of
dying, broke the taboo and threw open the subject to respectful,
concerned analysis.

   The inevitability and seeming finality of death shares with birth
the ultimate significance in human life. Increasing sensitivity to the
growth of personality to the very last moment of life has put focus on
the process of dying as one of high importance for human experience.
The new capacity of medical technology to lengthen physical existence
beyond full human consciousness has raised serious challenges to the
physician's right to determine existence, and the patient's "right to die"
(or "death with dignity") has become a crucial issue. The "death
industries" (funeral homes, legal wills, and a host of others) are being
challenged, and a secondary revolution in the rites of death is well
under way.

   The older dying person has been expected to assume a passive
acceptance of death, and gradually to relinquish control of existence

to family members, doctors, and other professionals. Hospice is only one of several movements designed to give control of life back to the dying person.

The role of religion and philosophy in the dying experience has always had importance. In our largely secular society, death is one area that remains closely tied to religion.

"I see death as a graduation exercise"—Elisabeth Kübler-Ross
"Death is the ultimate human task"—Lynn Caine

**On Death and Dying.** Elisabeth Kübler-Ross. New York: Macmillan, 1969. 260p.

This is the classic statement of the five stages of orientation to death and dying: denial, anger, bargaining, depression, and acceptance. As a psychiatrist, Kübler-Ross evolved this structure from her long experience with terminally ill cancer patients and from some 200 interviews with dying patients. Understanding of these stages by the patient and by families, friends, and physicians provides a safeguarding of the reality of death and allows maximum peace and personal dignity in the dying process.

Her other volumes amplify certain aspects of the dying: *Death: The Final Stage of Growth* (Englewood Cliffs, N.J.: Prentice-Hall, 1975. BRA 14540) and *To Live until We Say Good-bye* (Englewood Cliffs, N.J.: Prentice-Hall, 1978) with its emphasis on the peace that comes with acceptance.

**The Dying Patient.** Orville G. Brim and others. New York: Russell Sage, 1970. 390p. $12.95; New Brunswick, N.J.: Transaction Books, 1981. $9.95.

A series of papers focusing on the social context of dying, together with legal, ethical, and economic factors involved in the termination of life.

**Facing Death.** Robert E. Kavanaugh. New York: Penguin Books, 1974. 226p. $3.50.

An ex-priest, teacher, and counseling psychologist, Kavanaugh has specialized in problems of death and bereavement. His observations here cover the attitudes and customs related to death that need change, guilt feelings of survivors, use of therapy for grievers, and the meaning of funerals and cemeteries. Emphasis is on the seven stages of grief and their resolution.

**Making Today Count.** Orville E. Kelly. New York: Delacorte Press, 1975. 203p. $8.95; Paper 1975. $4.95.

Diagnosed as having terminal cancer, Kelly went through the now-traditional stages of anger, rejection, and depression before acceptance. His final constructive will to live led to his organization of people involved with terminal illness into "Make Today Count" mutual support groups. His personal life and his dying experience are briefly told, and an example of a meeting of the MTC group is detailed at the conclusion of this brief, readable book.

Az-BPH (AZ CB 678) RC

**The Jewish Way in Death and Mourning.** Maurice Lamm. Middle Village, N.Y.: Jonathan David, 1972. 224p. $5.95; Paper $4.95.

The author, a rabbi, presents to laymen the meaning and rites of death in the Jewish faith. Coverage of autopsies, choice of caskets, funeral services, burial, and obligations of mourners. Informed, simple guide.

**Why Survive? Being Old in America.** Robert N. Butler. New York: Harper & Row, 1975. 512p. $19.95; Paper $5.95.

Butler gives informed attention to the "right to die" and to the management of death (pp. 375-83).

**The Right to Die: A Neurosurgeon Speaks of Death with Candor.** Milton D. Heifetz and Charles Mangel. New York: Putnam's Sons, 1975. 234p.

The controversial issue of euthanasia discussed by a doctor who argues for the patient's right to die. Both ethical and legal aspects of euthanasia are dealt with.

**Last Rights.** Marya Mannes. New York: William Morrow, 1974. 150p.

The nature of death: good death, suicide, euthanasia. Claims that the right to choose death when life no longer holds meaning is the "last human right." Based on interviews with aged and dying persons, their families, doctors, and lawyers. Decries the use of "wonder drugs" to prolong a vegetable existence. Asks for legal validation of the patient's written request for euthanasia. Mannes's discussion may obscure some of the complexity and profundity of death.

Mi-BPH (MSL-4243) RM

**The Woman Said Yes: Encounters with Life and Death.** Jessamyn
West. New York: Harcourt, Brace, Jovanovich, 1976. 192p.
17.95; Paper. New York: Fawcett Book Group, 1977. $1.95;
Large Type. Boston: G. K. Hall, n.d. $10.95.

West affirms the value of life through her own fight against
tuberculosis and her support of her sister's preference for death over a
drug-dominated existence. Describes how she helped her beloved sister
escape a horrible death by cancer of the bowel by helping her commit
suicide. West also presented this in a fictional account: *A Matter of
Time.*

RD 09354

## PERSONAL EXPERIENCES
## OF DEATH

**A Death in the Sanchez Family.** Oscar Lewis. New York: Random
House, 1969. 119p. $7.95; Paper 1970. $2.95.

The death and funeral of old Aunt Guadalupe, as told by
members of the Sanchez family. Aunt Guadalupe's death illuminates
her life and reflects the culture of poverty in which she lived. Powerful
and affecting.

**Death's Single Privacy: Grieving and Personal Growth.** Joyce Phipps.
New York: Seabury Press, 1974. 143p.

Free of sentimentality and soundly based in a true sense of loss,
Phipps's account of the death of her husband and the practical and
human sympathy support in making the death real and in seeing life as
having new beginnings is a moving one. Based in Protestant religious
belief.

**The Summer of the Great Grandmother.** Madeleine L'Engle. New
York: Farrar, Straus and Giroux, 1974. 245p. $10.95; Paper.
New York: Seabury, 1980. $5.95.

An autobiographical account of the dying and death of the
author's mother at the summer home in a four-generation family. The
dying and the death were indeed the core and center of the summer's
experience for each person, but life and its multiple contexts pulses
throughout the narrative.

RC 09165

**A Very Easy Death.** Simone de Beauvoir. New York: Charles
Putnam, 1966. 106p.

A daughter (skilled and renowned author) recounts the
experience she and her sister shared in the final stages of their mother's
illness and death. The ambivalences of the mother/daughter
relationship, the generation gap, the wide disparity in emotional and
intellectual styles accentuate the basic close tie of the daughters to
their "full-blooded, spirited" parent, who seemed to them deformed
by her repressions and angry self-denials. De Beauvoir's reflections on
death as an experience and as a phenomenon will stimulate
perceptions and reflections in the educated reader. The author's
feelings of guilt and despair are pervasive. An easy death?

BR 01281

**A Death with Dignity: When the Chinese Came.** Lois Wheeler Snow.
New York: Random House, 1975. 148p.

Focus on the humanizing influence of the Chinese medical team
who came to Switzerland to be with Edgar Snow, their good friend,
during the final weeks of his dying with cancer.

**Autobiography of Dying.** Archie J. Hanlan. Garden City, N.Y.:
Doubleday, 1979. 193p. $8.95.

A social scientist, knowing of his impending death of Lou
Gehrig's disease, recorded his thoughts on death and dying over the
three-year period. The taped diary, with a postscript by his wife, is
vivid, direct, thought-provoking.

RC 15388

**Aging Is a Family Affair.** Victoria E. Bumagin and Kathryn F. Hirn.
New York: Thomas Crowell, 1979. 276p. $10.95.

The chapters on death, dying, and grief are direct, sympathetic,
and wise in counsel.

**The Art of Dying.** Robert E. Neale. New York: Harper & Row, 1973.
158p. $5.95.

An experiential text on death, dying, and grief. Transformation
of feelings and attitudes is the goal.

BRA 13276

**Leavetaking: When and How to Say Goodbye.** Mortimer R. Feinberg
and others. New York: Simon & Schuster, 1978. 286p.

"Death, the Last Leavetaking" is seen as farewells and losses both for the dying and for family and friends, and the pattern and strategy of leavetaking proposed for other human situations of loss are here applied with particular effectiveness to death.
RC 12083

**Living and Dying.** Robert Jay Lifton and Eric Olson. New York: Praeger, 1974. 156p.
The importance of death in the human life cycle from philosophical and sociological points of view. Distortion of the image of death by crime, the bomb, wars, mass starvation, and victimization is contrasted to the symbolizing of death in the human experience of nature, biology, and experiential transcendence.

**The Cost of Dying and What You Can Do about It.** Raymond Paavo Arvio. New York: Harper & Row, 1974. 159p.
Practical advice for formation of nonprofit memorial societies as an alternative to traditional funeral practices. Concerns of this sort have been widespread since the publication of Jessica Mitford's *The American Way of Death* (New York: Simon & Schuster, 1963) with its expose of the funeral industry, discussion of state laws and their misuse by the industry, the vulnerability of the bereaved, unnecessary expense, and so forth.

## PHILOSOPHIC AND RELIGIOUS BASES

**Spiritual Well-Being: Sociological Perspectives.** Edited by David C. Moberg. Lanham, Md.: University Press of America, 1979. 367p. $12.00.
Expanded from ideas in Moberg's 1971 White House Conference on Aging paper of the same title, this deals largely with religious beliefs and their importance in the life of the older adult, and with death, preparation for death, the right to die, belief in immortality. Judeo-Christian orientation.

**Love Is Stronger Than Death.** Peter J. Kreeft. New York: Harper & Row, 1979. 121p. $7.95.
What is death? Why do we die? The answers are deeply Christian and philosophical. A meditation on death.

**The Last Enemy: A Christian Understanding of Death.** Richard W. Doss. New York: Harper & Row, 1974. 104p.

Develops a Christian theology of death, and views spiritual renewal (a "resurrection") as the key to victory over death. Straightforward and compassionate, the book was written for the serious layman and the practicing minister.

**Coping with Death.** Robert A. Raab. New York: Richards Rosen Press, 1978. 128p. $7.95.

A rabbi's views on all of the problems concerned with death.

**A Mass for the Dead.** William Gibson. New York: Atheneum Publishers, 1968. 431p. $6.95.

Using the form of the Mass, Gibson provides a rich poetic appreciation of his parents in his reflection upon them in relation to himself and to his children, so that these dead parents rise with new meaning and vitality for him and he feels himself redeemed as a son, as a parent, as an artist.

BRA 02668; TB 12277

**Overcoming the Fear of Death.** David Cole Gordon. New York: Macmillan, 1970. 115p. $8.95.

Gordon sees the fear of death to be a fear of decay, of loss of self, of cessation of thought. Selfhood is seen as the major obstacle to acceptance of death and as obscuring mankind's underlying drive for unification with the universe.

**Living Your Dying.** Stanley Keleman. New York: Random House, 1976. 160p. $5.95.

Writing from the viewpoint of gestalt psychology, Keleman sees man as constrained by the traditional images of death and feels he needs to be freed to "die his own kind of death." He urges release of repressed fear, curiosity, anger, grief, and excitement about death so that we can plunge into the full experience of our feelings and—in time—the event itself.

**First American Hospice: Three Years of Home Care.** Sylvia A. Lack and Robert W. Buckingham III. New Haven, Conn.: Hospice, Inc., 1978. 281p. $15.75.

The objectives and procedures of hospice care in the context of patient and family needs during the period of terminal illness and dying. This manual gives great detail on these matters, not only to inform a beginning inquiry, but enough to assist in establishing a hospice service in a local community.

## Creative Literature

**Harold and Maude.** Colin Higgins. New York: Avon Books, 1975. 143p. $1.95.

A book of black humor and warm friendship, *Harold and Maude* probes death and dying from many perspectives. Harold, 21, and Maude, 69, meet at funerals which both attend for amusement. Out of their interest in death and mourning, a close friendship develops. Harold is melancholy and has attempted suicide many times for attention. While Maude is more lively and fun-loving than Harold, she is concerned about her own death. On her eightieth birthday she commits suicide so that she retains control over her death.

BR 01691; Film. Paramount, 1972.

**A Reckoning.** May Sarton. New York: W. W. Norton and Co., 1978. 245p. $11.95.

When Laura Spelman, 60, is told that she has inoperable cancer in both lungs, and only a short time to live, she is unexpectedly excited. "I am to have my own death." The process of stripping her life of "nonessentials" and of telling her mother, 80, three middle-aged children, and her two grandchildren, is sensitively and beautifully described. An excellent, moving book about dying, *A Reckoning* ends with Laura's death: "She had let go."

BR 04108

**"The Law of Life."** Jack London. In his *Best Short Stories of Jack London*, pp. 150-56. Garden City, N.Y.: Doubleday, 1953. $8.95; Paper. New York: Fawcett Book Group, 1978. $2.25.

Old Koskoosh is left to die in the snow when his tribe moves on. As is traditional, his son, the chief, and his granddaughter, Sit-am-to-ha, leave him a fire and a woodpile. Although he thanks them and tells them "It is well," he is resentful of their departure and frightened of death. As he slowly uses his wood supply, he reflects on life. "to perpetuate was the task of life; its law was death." He dies by a bullmoose at the end of this powerful story. "What did it matter after all? Was it not the law of life?"

**"Do Not Go Gentle."** Dylan Thomas. In his *Collected Poems*, p. 128. New York: New Directions, 1971. $4.75.

Thomas wrote this famous poem to his dying father, exhorting him to reject despair and resignation in the face of death. "Do not go gentle into that good night,/Old age should burn and rave at close of day."

BR 03250

Another famous poem on death, this one with a different point of view, is "Terminus" by Ralph Waldo Emerson (BRA 15167). Old age is welcome, as is death. Emerson portrays both as positive experiences. "It is time to be old,/To take in sail..../The port, well worth the cruise, is near,/And every wave is charmed."

**"White to Move."** William Brower. *Short Story International* 3(14): 149-64, June 1979.

Chess is all that matters to Ira Bennett, who is dying in a hospital. When he learns that Sergius Jelinsky, a famous chess master, is a patient in the same hospital, he challenges him to a game. Ira spends his seventy-eighth birthday playing the last chess game of his life.

BR 03250

**"There Was an Old Woman."** Ray Bradbury. In his *October Country*, pp. 249-64. New York: Knopf, 1970. 272p. $10.00; New York: Ballantine Books, 1975.

Old Aunt Tildy is visited by a tall dark man with a coffin for her. She refuses to go with him, but he steals her body. Tildy goes to the funeral parlor and insists on their returning her body to her. When they agree, she steps back into it and lives on—even showing the autopsy scar to visitors. This fantasy tale may be a good discussion starter on the subject of death.

TB 00852

**Praise the Human Season.** Don Robertson. New York: Ballantine Books, 1975. 640p. $1.95.

Anne Amberson is dying of breast cancer when her husband, Howard, decides that they should take an automobile trip to "find the meaning of the apparatus." He is ill, also, with heart disease, but the two enjoy their adventures. At the end of the novel, she dies in a motel room and he decides to join her. Knowing that his heart will not be able to withstand it, he goes running, happy in his decision.

RC 11372

**"The Jilting of Granny Weatherall."** Katherine Anne Porter. In *The Collected Short Stories of Katherine Anne Porter*, pp. 80-89. New York: New American Library, 1979. $4.95.

Eighty-year-old Granny Weatherall is dying, surrounded by her loving children. But she can't keep herself from thinking about George, the man who jilted her 60 years before. She has prided herself on her hard work and her family; also on her ability to forget (but not forgive) him. Now, at the end, she feels jilted twice: by her memory and by the priest who is not there when she needs him.

Film. American Short Story Series, PBS, 1980.

**"A Special Occasion."** Patricia Zelver. In her *A Man of Middle Age and Twelve Stories*, pp. 169-76. New York: Holt, Rinehart and Winston, 1980. 228p. $12.95.

After his third stroke, Mr. Moore, 88, knows that he is dying. He feels that death is an occasion and should be observed as an important landmark; he feels that his last words should be heard and recorded. But the nurses, his daughter, and his sons tell him not to be morbid, that he is not dying. Only his eight-year-old granddaughter, Gilly, allows him to feel that his death is meaningful and important, as he answers her direct and honest questions about death.

**"To Hell with Dying."** Alice Walker. In her *In Love and Trouble*, pp. 129-38. New York: Harcourt, Brace, Jovanovich, 1974. 138p. $2.65; In *We Are but a Moment's Sunlight*, pp. 80-87. Edited by Charles S. Adler. New York: Pocket Books, 1976. $1.95.

A young woman recalls Mr. Sweet, an elderly alcoholic guitar player who lived near her family, and the many times she and her siblings rescued him from death by their love. Whenever he was ill, her father would say, "To Hell with dying ... these children want Mr. Sweet." The children would throw themselves on his bed, and kiss and tickle him until he revived. But at 24, the narrator is recalled from college for Mr. Sweet's birthday, on which he died. Nobody was able to revive him that time. He left her his guitar and memories.

**Tell Me a Riddle.** Tillie Olsen. New York: Dell Publishing Co., 1978. $8.95; Paper 1976. $2.25.

Parts 2 and 4 of this novella center on Ma's dying. After her hospitalization for cancer, Pa convinces her to visit her children and grandchildren whom she cannot warm up to. "If they would but leave her ... to journey to her self." She is weary of having to care for people and to worry about their well-being. In part 4 she dies while she and Pa are living with the one grandchild who understands her.

Film. Godmother Productions, 1980.

**The Death of a Nobody.** Jules Romains. New York: Howard Fertig, Inc., 1974. 137p. $15.95.

Jacques Godard, a retired railroad man, dies unexpectedly after eight days of a fever. But he is more alive now in the discussions of his neighbors, relatives, colleagues, and even strangers. Romains's theme is "People don't make so much about you when you're alive." His death also brings life to a group of people who otherwise didn't know each other (e.g., the people in his building who must plan his funeral). Very readable and provides a good basis for discussion.

**Memento Mori.** Muriel Spark. New York: Time, 1964. 246p.

Dame Lettie Colston receives anonymous telephone calls in which a male voice cautions her: "Remember you must die." Soon her friends and relatives receive similar calls and the police are alerted. It is clear that the calls are from Death and that the characters, all of whom are elderly, are preoccupied with mortality.

TB 02953

# TASKS
# OF
# OPPORTUNITY

Aging in our society offers rich opportunities for intensive, exhilarating living. Up to the 1980s in the United States, the twentieth century has awarded older adults in increasingly large numbers a larger measure of leisure with its opportunities for new experience and growth. Aging in itself provides the opportunity for fresh perspectives and new insights, and that is one of its chief rewards; this spurs creativity and intellectual growth. The forced self-reappraisal, which role changes involve, gives the opportunity for self-affirmation and self-realization beyond the stereotypical models of middle age. The breadth of world understanding with new perspectives on time, on the human family, on the structure of the universe (philosophic, religious, or scientific) are enhanced in the 1980s by the tremendous growth in knowledge and its accessibility to the layman in books and the media. "Keeping current" is one of the exciting, demanding tasks of aging — filling in the gaps in personal knowledge and keeping abreast of the enormous developments in the sciences and in human affairs. Inner growth is spurred by the search for resolution of old, incompleted problems or griefs, for expanded human experience in literature and the arts, and for spiritual well-being. Other expression of that inner self comes in artistic creativity, in community service, in family and friendship tie-binding, and in political action.

The expression of these tasks of opportunity are found in classical literature, in biography and autobiography, and in current gerontological literature written for the layman. Poetry, fiction, and drama of our times reflect the insight that old age provides rich and intensive living in the final phase of life.

# LEISURE

Leisure involves a transformation of activities from a focus on work and productivity to a focus on pleasure or "pleasuring" as a way of life marked by spontaneity, freedom, and voluntary activity, by experiencing rather than by achieving. The Greek concept of leisure was the cultivation of the mind, of learning, and of exercising reason, of gaining perceptions and wisdom. In our society in the mid-twentieth century, leisure has tended to mean "good times," fun, recreation. With the increase in the number of better-educated people in retirement years in the 1970s, however, leisure has come to have a wider meaning than "good times," and looks to the Greek concept of leisure as a meaningful model.

For generations, pleasure in our society has seemed to have had to be earned in order to be indulged in without guilt. Yet the heart of "pleasuring" (whether in physical, social, or intellectual activities) arises within the sense of freedom, of voluntary choice, of enjoyment for its own sake. Many older adults may have to relearn the childhood art of joyous play, the capacity for pleasure without guilt. Dangott and Kalish, in *A Time to Enjoy*, devote a full chapter to this topic of pleasure in leisure in older years.

**A Time to Enjoy: The Pleasures of Aging.** Lillian R. Dangott and Richard A. Kalish. Englewood Cliffs, N.J.: Prentice-Hall, 1978. 182p. $11.95; Paper $4.95.

An introduction to aging as a phase of growth focusing on self-actualization. Challenging the past stereotypes, Dangott and Kalish speak to adults in middle and later years. Useful guidance on exercise, diet, stress, biofeedback, grief and mourning, death and dying. The final chapter, "The Pleasures of Aging," is the unique contribution of this excellent book, with discussion of leisure theory, "pleasuring," and personal fulfillment in older age.

**Life Begins at Fifty.** Walter B. Pitkin, Jr. New York: Simon & Schuster, 1965. 224p.

Echoing his father's *Life Begins at Forty* published in 1932, the son speaks to the current generation whose middle age and aging comes at least 10 years later. Case studies and fictional personal histories focus on the richly rewarding later years made possible by planning ahead for retirement. Readable, informal book that highlights the enjoyment of life.

BRA 09795

**In the Fullness of Time.** Avis D. Carlson. South Bend, Ind.: Henry Regnery, 1977. 195p.; Large Type. South Yarmouth, Mass.: John Curley & Associates, 1979. $10.95.

At the age of 80, Carlson looks back over the aging experience and finds the skills, techniques, and attitudes that make possible a positive, mature aging.

RD 11801

**The Old Ones of New Mexico.** Robert Coles. Albuquerque: University of New Mexico Press, 1973. 74p. $7.95.

Some extraordinary old people talk about themselves and their lives in rural northern New Mexico. Poor, they have to work harder than many people half their age, but to them work is beautiful; they have put leisuring into life.

**Never Too Late.** John Holt. New York: Delacorte Press, 1978. 245p. $10.00; Paper 1980. $4.95.

Educator John Holt recounts with delight the flowering of his musical career which he began after the age of 40. This autobiographical account is lightened by personal anecdote and good humor throughout. Those with interest in the learning process and in music will find this especially engaging reading. Holt represents an adult with the skills of leisuring!

**Threshold: The First Days of Retirement.** Alan H. Olmstead. New York: Harper & Row, 1975. 214p. $8.95; Large Type. Boston: G. K. Hall, 1977. $12.50.

These brief, manicured two-page essays in day-to-day journal style include a delightful and perceptive one on leisure (pp. 212-13). The book as a whole reflects the progress of a man moving himself from a work orientation to a leisure orientation.

**These Rich Years: A Journal of Retirement.** Jean and Robert Hersey. New York: Charles Scribner & Sons, 1969. 270p.

The ambience of relaxed leisure spiced with adventure and moments of daring is projected by this upper middle class couple as good retirement living. Warm relationships between them and with their friends are part of the product of that leisuring approach to living.

BRA 01516

**Successful Aging.** Olga Knopf. New York: Viking Press, 1975. 229p. $8.95; Large Type. Boston: G. K. Hall, 1977. $12.50.

A practical guide to the experience of growing older, this contains a full discussion (chapter 6) on the use of leisure time. Similarly, Lillian E. Troll and Joan and Kenneth Israel, in their *Looking Ahead: A Woman's Guide to the Problems and Joys of Growing Older* (Prentice-Hall, 1977), devote chapter 11 to a discussion of women and leisure.

**You Are Never Too Old to Learn.** Wilbur Cross and Carol Florio. New York: McGraw-Hill, 1978. 226p. $5.50.

Learning is a lifelong process, and leisure opens new opportunities for extension of this pleasurable activity. Cross and Florio offer full lists of resources and styles of learning.

**"Aging in Humanistic Perspective."** Walter Moss. In his *Humanistic Perspectives on Aging: An Annotated Bibliography and Essay.* Ann Arbor, Mich.: Institute of Gerontology, 1976, pp. 1-6.

Moss gives a delightful, unpretentious but sophisticated interpretation of the opportunities in leisure for growth and life appreciation for older adults through literature and the literary arts.

**In Praise of Seasons.** Alan Olmstead. New York: Harper & Row, 1977. 87p. $6.95.

A man in retirement reports on his relationship with garden, soil and hill, with sky and bird and weather. The true capture of leisuring in nature.

## Creative Literature

**"A Cross Country Runner at 65."** Paul Goodman. In *Adam and His Works: Collected Stories of Paul Goodman*, pp. 188-99. New York: Random House, 1968. 438p.

Perry Westover, 65, is an institution in the Winchester Borough Cross-Country Race, the oldest race in the state. He has run in it all 45 times and has won 5 times. Although his family, except for his youngest grandson, thinks he is too old to continue running, he is determined to continue the sport which gives his life meaning.

**The Golden Years Caper.** Robert Carson. Boston: Little, Brown and
    Co., 1970. 243p.

Bored with their lives in Golden Years, Inc. (a large senior
housing complex), a group of residents commit "illegal adventures"
under the direction of Grandma Bandit. They call themselves The
Seniles and the media enjoy publicizing their escapades, especially the
kidnapping of a famous recording artist, since they always outwit the
police.

**Ahmed and the Old Lady.** Jon Godden. New York: Knopf, 1976.
    203p.; Large Type. Boston: G. K. Hall, 1977. $11.50.

With her husband dead and her grandson off at war, Leah
Harding, 80, goes to India. She is finally free to take a mountain trek
in Kashmir, to fulfill a lifelong dream. Despite protests that she is too
old, she hires a personal servent, Ahmed, as well as guides and
equipment, and starts the journey. An adventure story complete with
criminal servants and physical danger, this is a good portrayal of a
strong older woman. Leah contracts pneumonia and dies in the
mountains with Ahmed by her side.

BR 03141

In another Godden novel about travel, 79-year-old Isa
Panapoulis takes one last sea voyage with her niece and paid
companion, Flora (*Mrs. Panapoulis.* New York: Knopf, 1959. 205p.).
Mrs. Panapoulis is a feisty, strong, independent woman, out to enjoy
herself and marry off her niece.

**"The Golden Honeymoon."** Ring Lardner. In *Fifty Best American
    Short Stories 1915-1965*, pp. 23-77. Edited by Martha Foley
    and David Burnett. Boston: Houghton Mifflin, 1965. 814p.
    $15.00.

Lucy and Charley go on a golden honeymoon to celebrate their
fiftieth anniversary. Charley tells the story of their encounter with
Frank, an old suitor of hers, and of the rest of their vacation travel.

**Travels with My Aunt.** Graham Greene. New York: Viking Press,
    1970. 324p. $14.95; New York: Penguin Books, 1977. $2.95.

At his mother's funeral, Henry Pulling is reacquainted with his
75-year-old aunt. Augusta Bertram is an eccentric woman who has
always been presented as his aunt but is really his mother. A schemer
and world traveler, she persuades Henry, who is a sedate retired
banker, to accompany her on her escapades. A humorous, satiric
novel about a fiery old woman, happy with her past and her present.

BR 01253; RD 14936; Film. Metro-Goldwyn-Mayer Ltd., 1972.

**Sadie Shapiro in Miami.** Robert Kimmel Smith. New York: Simon & Schuster, 1977. 189p.; Paper. New York: Fawcett Book Group, 1978; Large Type. Boston: G. K. Hall, 1978.

Celebrity, author, and famous knitter, Sadie Shapiro (72 or 75, depending on whose story you believe) endorses Senior World. Designed as a Disneyland for older people, Senior World is to highlight old movies and live performance while providing services such as a health clinic, low sodium foods, etc. When the planner absconds with the money, Sadie and her husband and friends save the project. Sadie is eccentric, lovable, and funny; so is the novel, which is written in the sentence structure and cadence of Yiddish speakers. The theme of leisure time is presented both through Senior World (see her reaction on pp. 143-44) and through Sadie's own life.

RC 12358

This is a sequel to *Sadie Shapiro's Knitting Book* (New York: Simon & Schuster, 1973), in which Sadie became famous for her leisure activities, knitting, and jogging, and shared her adventures with the other persons in her senior residence.

# CREATIVITY AND INTELLECTUAL GROWTH

Creativity is the key to good aging, says John McLeish in *The Ulyssean Adult*. He sees creativity as a natural human process, not dependent upon special talents (although using whatever is available). As a process, it represents the interaction between the unique individual and the "materials, events, people, or circumstances of his/her life" (p. 34). Spontaneous, open, zestful forms of activity give a product unique to the person and the occasion. Problem solving, human networking, rearing of children, household management, all use creativity — the investment of the unique quality of the actor in the situation. This, says McLeish, is the key to good old age. Biography and autobiography abundantly illustrate the diverse areas in which creativity is expressed.

Intellectual growth is a matter of both acquiring new knowledge and of reprocessing what is known in the light of experience. Both processes open great opportunity to older adults. Curiosity is a basic human drive; learning — for those whose curiosity is high — has become a way of life. As leisure increases, those who have found learning satisfying are free to indulge intensively.

Beyond curiosity as a motive, there are many life tasks that can be better met by "finding out" about them, in advance of their occurrence or at least at the moment of crisis. Such learning is goal-oriented and meets important personal needs. Further, the process of learning is a pleasant one for many people, leading to new and rewarding social contacts and activities. It is a happy lifestyle. In short, learning has many ways of enhancing one's resources for living.

**The Ulyssean Adult: Creativity in the Middle and Later Years.** John A. B. McLeish. Toronto: McGraw-Hill Ryerson, Ltd., 1976. 309p. $12.50.

The purpose of this book is to change one's attitudes toward the later years so that they become a vital part of life, to be anticipated and enjoyed, to be lived positively and creatively. For those who have succumbed to negative images of aging and limiting social conventions about older adults, this is a counter response! Rich in case illustrations and literary examples. "To strive, to seek, to find, and not to yield!"

**Second Chance: Blueprints for Life Change.** Herbert B. Livesay. Philadelphia: J. B. Lippincott, 1977. 238p.

Brief biographical sketches of a great diversity of people who lived creatively, who saw a "second chance" and took it, even late in life! Highly readable anecdotal approach to the potentials that life offers at any stage.

**What's Inside You, It Shines Out of You.** Marc Kaminsky. New York: Horizon Press, 1974. 236p.; Paper 1977. $5.95.

The title of this book came from a member of an older adult poetry group taught by Kaminsky. Through reading poetry to the group and encouraging them to write their own, Kaminsky stimulated the creativity that endows the poetry quoted from the group with feeling, dignity, and courage.

Kenneth Koch's *I Never Told Anybody: Teaching Poetry Writing in a Nursing Home* (New York: Random House, 1977) is a similar sharing of experience and technique in stimulating creativity among groups of older adults for whom this was a novel experience. The rich rewards of creativity in later years is fully documented in these two volumes.

**Foxfire Books.** Edited by Eliot Wigginton. Garden City, N.Y.: Doubleday, 1975-1980. Set Books 1-3. 1312p. $20.85; Set Books 4-6. 1520p. $20.85; also available individually.

Older adults in the mountain communities of North Carolina share with student interviewers the lore of ghost stories, of spotting wild plant foods, of spinning and weaving, midwifing, burial customs, and more affairs of plain living. The zest that comes with sharing important knowledge is a kind of creativity that fills these pages.

**Grandma Moses: Favorite Painter.** Charles Graves. Champaign, Ill.: Garrard Publishing Company, 1969. 96p. $6.48.

A simple biography of the well-known artist who began painting at the age of 76 and had a 24-year career. The spirit of creativity in a rural New York setting.

**Out of My Life and Thought: An Autobiography.** Albert Schweitzer. New York: Holt, Rinehart and Winston, 1949. 274p.

The remarkable creativity of the man as physician, theologian, musician, and humanitarian seems somehow to explain his monumental status and his long, productive life. A man in balance! Simplicity, honesty, humility, humor mark his account of his life.

BRA 01147; BRA 11317; TB 01115

Norman Cousins reported in *Dr. Schweitzer of Lambarene* (New York: Harper & Row, 1960) an account of his trip to French Equatorial Africa to photograph Schweitzer's last uncompleted manuscripts (lest the originals be lost) and to secure a taping of Schweitzer's unequivocal rejection of atomic warfare. An intimate and human presentation of Schweitzer in vigorous old age.

**You Are Never Too Old to Learn.** Wilbur Cross and Carol Florio. New York: McGraw-Hill, 1978. 226p. $5.50.

In an easy, popular style addressed to high school or college graduates now in their sixties, seventies, or eighties, Cross and Florio provide information on a wide range of learning opportunities. The key concept in the book (elaborated in chapter 5) is that "an objective can change your life." Learning and education are built around individually chosen objectives, whether to meet the tasks of aging or to understand changes in the world about us, or to pursue individual interests. As one of their interviewees commented: "If I live to be 110, I'll never be able to take all the courses that interest me."

**Never Too Late.** John Holt. New York: Delacorte Press, 1978. 245p. $10.00; Paper 1980. $4.95.

John Holt, educator, analyzes his own learning experience in becoming a cellist after age 40. He reports with appreciation the two paths he followed: learning from charismatic model-setting teachers of the cello and intensive self-instruction. His account makes fascinating his choice of study styles.

**How to Read a Book.** Rev. ed. Mortimer J. Adler and Charles Van Doren. New York: Simon & Schuster, 1972. 426p. $5.95.

An engaging and engrossing manual on reading skills and the basic styles of reading necessary to learning: scanning, inspectional reading, analytical reading, and syntopical reading. Stimulates intellectual explorations in many directions.

RD 06047

**Looking Ahead: A Woman's Guide to the Problems and Joys of Growing Older.** Lillian E. Troll and Joan and Kenneth Israel. Englewood Cliffs, N.J.: Prentice-Hall, 1977. 216p. $9.95; Paper $3.95.

Chapters 14 and 15 provide guidance into learning as a lifestyle: "Lifelong Learning" and "Education as Recreation."

## *Creative Literature*

**Mrs. Stevens Hears the Mermaids Singing.** May Sarton. New York: W. W. Norton, 1974. 240p. $6.95; Paper 1975. $3.95.

Two young reporters interview Hilary Stevens, a famous 70-year-old poet, about her life and her work. During the interview (part 3 of the novel) Hilary crystallizes her opinions on the muse and on creativity. A portrayal of a strong, creative, introspective older woman.

**"The Bedquilt."** Dorothy Canfield Fisher. In her *Hillsboro People*, pp. 61-68. New York: Henry Holt & Co., 1915. 346p.

Aunt Mehitabel, 68, lives with her relatives, helping with the chores and staying out of the way. The unmarried, dependent woman is accustomed to being taken for granted and ignored. Her only joy, her only work for herself, and her only claim to notice is her quilting. An inspired new pattern gives her pleasure in the making and a surprise in the result. For once, she is recognized for her work and is given a place—and time—to work on her beloved quilting. The quilt is entered in the county fair and wins first prize. More important, 68-year-old Mehitabel goes to the fair, which is farther from home than she has ever been.

**The Horse's Mouth.** Joyce Cary. New York: Harper & Row, 1965. $2.25.

Gulley Jimson, artist and rogue, in his late years is still moved by the compulsions to create art, whether the tempestuous sunset on canvas or thousands of human feet on the dining room wall of his friend's home. For the delightful duration of the novel, the reader sees the world with new eyes.

BRA 04644; TB 02358

# SELF-AFFIRMATION AND SELF-ACTUALIZATION

Self-affirmation is the first major task of later years; one must be able to see oneself as important and worthy beyond the world of work or family-related responsibilities. As one retires, sees one's adult children become independent, watches family and friends loosen some of their mutual dependence through life changes, the reaffirmation of the self for what the self represents becomes of major importance. Tennyson has Ulysses say "I am a part of all that I have met."

Mental health in older years is closely tied to the warmly accepting social environment, a society that regards old age as worthy, dignified, and as having a positive social value. Self-affirmation among older adults, then, may be seen not only as a goal for survival of the older person as an individual but also as a contribution to the creation of social acceptance of older adults as worthy people.

Gail Sheehy in *Passages* (New York: Dutton, 1978) identifies (p. 509) a "disassembling period" through which one moves toward renewal of integrity and self-affirmation. Often this is accomplished by changes in lifestyle, and Sheehy concludes that the courage to take new steps, to seek new satisfactions and responses, will release the richness of the next stage of life.

Self-actualization, according to Abraham Maslow in *Motivation and Personality* (New York: Harper & Row, 1970), refers to the full development of a person's human potential. Such fulfillment, says Maslow, most typically occurs among older adults in the growth of mind and spirit. The later years are those well-structured to enable this level of self-actualization. Eric Erikson's eight life stages reserved to older adults the stage of "integrity vs. despair," seeing the adult as either satisfied with his life, his accomplishments, with what he has done and become (therefore to be in a state of "integrity") or depressed and unhappy, emphasizing failures and fears. The task of self-affirmation and self-actualization in the late years focuses here. Robert Peck, adapting Erikson's eighth stage, says work-role preoccupation gives way to self-redefinition and reappraisal as the major task.

**Aging.** Henri J. M. Nouwen and Walter J. Gaffney. Photographs by Ron P. Van den Bosch. Garden City, N.Y.: Doubleday and Company, 1974. 152p.; Paper $2.45.

A psychologist-priest writes a poetic essay on aging as the gradual fulfillment of the life cycle. Recognizing the losses and stresses associated with aging, Nouwen focuses on the warmth, caring, and human richness that aging can bring to life through greater understanding of ourselves.

**The View from Eighty.** Malcolm Cowley. New York: Viking Press, 1980. 96p. $6.95; Paper. Penguin Books, 1982. $3.85; Large Type. Boston: G. K. Hall, 1981. $9.95.

Author and critic, Cowley has reached into the book realm (Emerson, Yeats, Gogarty, Cicero, Scott-Maxwell, de Beauvoir and many others) for the phrasing and concepts that state the view of life from the age of 80. He brings his own challenging statement of issues as well: "Among the vices of old age are avarice, untidiness, and vanity"; "one's 80th birthday is a time for thinking about the future, not the past"; "the aging person may undergo an identity crisis ... they yearn for recognition of what they have been."

BR 04729; RD 15814; RC 15814

**With Wings as Eagles.** Perry D. Gresham. Winter Park, Fla.: Anna Publishing Company, 1980. 275p. $10.95; Paper $5.95; Large Type.

A retired college president, Gresham at 73 a traveler and lecturer, here presents his perspective on the potential of the later years for creativity and regeneration. In his informally conversational text, Gresham deals both with psychological orientations in the Judeo-Christian tradition and with such practical matters as health and human relations that underlie the capacity to use the post-retirement years to "mount up with wings as eagles."

**Vintage: The Bold Survivors!** Jean Dufault. New York: Pilgrim Press, 1978. 256p. $12.95.

Thirty-eight life profiles, drawing seasoned commentary from across the world from those rich in years and living: English painter,

Alabama farmer, retired American professor living in Florida, a lemon vendor in Nice, and so forth. Superb photographic portraits and excellently edited text make this an international mosaic in self-realization.

**Living Longer and Loving It.** Deborah Geller and Arthur Geller. Maplewood, N.J.: Hammond, 1979. 184p. $7.95.

Upbeat, joyous, self-actualizing older adults, the 37 men and women interviewed for these profiles reflect the various channels chosen to enrich living after retirement: new careers, learning, political activism, senior center participation, the arts, remarriage. Fresh, candid stories of real lives.

**Your Second Life: Vitality in Middle and Later Age.** Gay Gaer Luce. New York: Delacorte Press, 1979. 465p. $10.95.

"Improving the quality of experience and consciousness in later age" is cited as the goal of SAGE (Senior Actualization and Growth Explorations), which this book presents. The premises of SAGE (pp. 7-8) are: old age is the time for self-development and spiritual growth; people need challenge, guidance, support, and deep emotional nourishment for growth; growth and well-being are enhanced by pleasurable experience; each person is unique and will unfold in his or her own way; many of the ailments of age are reversible; old age can be a time of emancipation and a time of truth. SAGE started in 1974 under the guidance of Gay Luce, psychologist and social worker in an eclectic evolution incorporating nutrition, massage, art therapy, bioenergetics, Sufi dancing, psychic development, meditation, and so forth. This is the manual that tells how it is done.

A briefer introduction to SAGE is Karen Preuss's *Life Time: A New Image of Aging* (Santa Cruz: Unity Press, 1978). This presents in photograph and text some of the exercises and group dialogues to provide an initial experience.

**The New Art of Living.** Norman Vincent Peale. New York: Fawcett Book Group, 1977. 160p. $2.50.

This new edition of Peale's first *Art of Living* includes new illustrations and references that provide ways to deal with the fear, tension, guilt, loneliness, and negativisms in our time. Comparable, but lacking the updating, are the still-relevant *The Mind Alive* by Harry and Bonaro Overstreet (New York: W. W. Norton, 1954) and Harry Emerson Fosdick's *On Being a Real Person* (New York: Harper & Brother, 1943) which have become classics, serving beyond the generation to which they were specifically addressed. Philosophic psychological insights grounded in the Judeo-Christian thought of mid-twentieth century, these books have led thousands of adults on the road to self-affirmation and self-actualization.

**Your Erroneous Zones.** Wayne W. Dyer. New York: Funk & Wagnalls/Thomas Y. Crowell, 1976. 256p. $10.95; Paper. New York: Avon Books, 1981. $2.75.

Bold but simple techniques for taking charge of unhealthy behavior patterns (guilt, fear of the unknown, anger, worry, and so forth). Broad appeal and currency.

RD 09562

**Self-Creation.** George Weinberg. New York: St. Martin's Press, 1978. 228p. $8.95; Paper. New York: Avon Books, 1978. $2.50.

Dr. Weinberg, psychiatrist, holds that our behavior reinforces our feelings and that what we do daily creates us as we are. A challenge to change through positive actions to improve your life.

RD 11720

**A High Old Time: Or How to Enjoy Being a Woman over Sixty.** Lavinia Russ. New York: Saturday Review Press, 1972. 140p.; Large Type. Boston: G. K. Hall, 1972. $6.95.

Sprightly, practical, amusing guide to life after 60 written by a housewife, grandmother, traveler, saleswoman, fashion stylist, book reviewer, TV commentator! One hundred ways to avoid waking up in the morning to face a day with nothing to do.

RC 07886

**More Than Mere Survival: Conversations with Women over 65.** Jane Seskin. New York: Newsweek Books, 1980. 296p. $8.95.

Looking for role models? Twenty-two women who have remained growing, active people: a state Supreme Court justice, a sculptor, an advertising executive, Maggie Kuhn of Grey Panthers, a trailer camp resident, or Hildegarde, the supper club entertainer. Vigorous women who take life in stride at 65, 78, or 92!

**Retirement: Creating Promise Out of Threat.** Robert K. Kinzel. New York: American Management Association AMACOM, 1979. 131p. $12.95.

Based on research with men in middle and upper management, this guide to personal decisions in later years is clearly for the middle to upper middle income populations. Chatty, well-focused manual that reflects Kinzel's skills as a counselor. Social integration, self-respect, and satisfying activities based on self-understanding. Brief, perceptive, this guide might serve as a basis for retirement discussion groups as well as for individual counseling.

**Learn to Grow Old.** Paul Tournier. New York: Harper & Row, 1973. 256p. $10.95.

The realization of the self in the new context of aging, with relinquishment of power and the cultivation of spirit, is Tournier's theme. Delightful leisurely reading. See also Abraham Maslow's *Motivation and Personality* (New York: Harper, 1970) for the chapter on "Self-actualizing People: A Study of Psychological Health."
RD 06591

**Journal of a Solitude, 1970-1971.** May Sarton. New York: W. W. Norton, 1973. 208p. $11.95; Paper. 1977. $3.95; Large Type. Boston: G. K. Hall, 1979. $13.95.

Third in what has now become a longer series of personal diaries through which May Sarton has revealed herself to her readers. Responsive to literature, flowers, music, the moods of weather that sweep her Maine seascape, Sarton relies on solitude as respite from intense living and as time to put it all together. Part of the mounting search for self-understanding.
Nj-B (C1472m) RC

Florida Scott-Maxwell's *Measure of My Days* (New York: Knopf, 1968) and Eleanor Roosevelt's *Autobiography* (New York: Harper & Row, 1961) are two special contributions to the literature of self-understanding and self-actualization.

## Creative Literature

**"A Man of Middle Age."** Patricia Zelver. In her *A Man of Middle Age and Twelve Stories*, pp. 1-69. New York: Holt, Rinehart and Winston, 1980. 228p. $12.95.

At 57, Sam Winkle (né Winklestein) decides to quit his job in advertising and open his own business. An upper middle-class suburbanite who has enjoyed his life the way it is, Sam is disturbed by the many changes around him. His wife, Alice, is studying to be a realtor; his daughter, Cindy, is traveling around the world to learn the meaning of life; the new management at his agency wants things done differently; and his new neighbors are an embarrassment. These disruptions of his routine make Sam reconsider and reaffirm his own life.

**"Old Mr. Marblehall."** Eudora Welty. In *Collected Stories of Eudora Welty*, pp. 91-97. New York: Harcourt, Brace, Jovanovich, 1980. 576p. $17.50.

Described through the eyes of the town's residents, Mr. Marblehall at 66 is feeble, old, and on his way to the grave. Actually, he has started two new lives since his sixtieth birthday—he has married two women and started two families, one named Bird and one named Marshall. He feels that he has finally learned how to "store up life," and to disregard the sneering and condescension of his neighbors who have no idea about his secret lives.

RC 16598

**The Gin Game.** D. L. Coburn. New York: Drama Book Specialists, 1978. 73p. $7.95.

Weller Martin is enraged that Fonsia Dorsey always beats him at gin rummy. They play daily at the Bentley Nursing and Convalescent Home, where they pretend that their status is better than it is. But during one of their games, their discussion becomes heated and they come to realizations about themselves and each other.

BR 04241; RD 14023

**"The Flight of Betsey Lane."** Sarah Orne Jewett. In her *The Country of the Pointed Firs and Other Stories*. Garden City, N.Y.: Doubleday, 1954. 320p.

Betsey Lane, who at 69 is the youngest resident of Byfleet Poor Farm, has wanted to go to the Centennial. When a visitor unexpectedly gives her some money, she hordes it until she can sneak away for nine glorious days of excitement. She returns, bearing souvenirs for all of her friends at the home.

RC 16145

**"Mrs. Ripley's Trip."** Hamlin Garland. In his *Main Travelled Roads*, pp. 167-79. New York: New American Library, 1962. 271p. $1.95.

Mrs. Ripley surprises her husband and the whole town when she decides to return to New York for her first visit from the Iowa plains in 23 years. She says that she is tired of sticking "to the churn and stove," and leaves on her adventure.

TB 01036

**"The Cathedral Builder."** Louis Auchincloss. In his *Second Chances*, pp. 19-42. Boston: Houghton-Mifflin Co., 1970. 262p.

John Lancaster's father had been one of the original fundraisers for the St. Matthew's Cathedral, begun 70 years before. Now John decides to use his personal fortune to finish it. At 89, his single passion is the cathedral's completion; he wants (needs) to see it completed during his lifetime. But even his money is not enough for this vast project, and he dies before it is done.

**All Passion Spent.** V. Sackville-West. Garden City, N.Y.: Sun Dial Press, Inc., 1931. 294p.

When Lord Slane (Henry Holland) dies at 94, his 88-year-old widow, Viceraine, dramatically changes her life. She realizes that she had been the devoted wife only at the expense of her own career as a painter. Pages 191-217 describe a visit she has from an old friend who had secretly loved her for many years. Her discussions with him, as well as with two new friends she makes, convince her to carry out the rest of her life as she wants. This includes rejecting an inherited fortune, not seeing her children, and living alone with a servant. At the end of this excellent novel, she dies happy with her new identity.

# SPIRITUAL WELL-BEING

Spiritual well-being, as defined by David O. Moberg in his 1971 White House Conference on Aging paper on this topic, pertains to man's inner resources, ultimate concerns, and basic values (p. 3) and thus becomes a source of life and guide to conduct. Search for meaningful goals in later years frequently focuses on a "quiet life-style with greater self-control and lessened compulsion to produce and compete, and with increased pleasure in the success and accomplishments of others" (T. B. Robb, *The Bonus Years*, 1968, as quoted in Moberg, p. 13). Wisdom, maturity, and spirituality are used to describe this way of life. Personal development continues throughout life and even the final hours before death may bring such great transformation as Tolstoi envisioned in his short story "The Death of Ivan Ilyich." Elisabeth Kübler-Ross's account of dying has documented the high significance of the final phases of dying.

As a final phase of self-actualization, perhaps, Robert C. Peck identifies body transcendence and ego transcendence as major tasks of older years. Peck and others see transcendence as a basic human need in later years, both body transcendence (the capacity to rise above the limitations of failing physical powers to attain a sense of health and wholeness) and ego transcendence (attaining a sense of self-actualization through a world or universal perspective less closely tied to ego demands and self-image). The capacity for transcendence seems to come, at least in part, from the very changes in bodily powers and in roles of power and control as the older person relinquishes his tight ego control. Religion and philosophy, as well as creative literature, are the paths by which such transcendence often comes. (See John McLeish's discussion of transcendence in *The Ulyssean Adult*, pp. 80-91.) Peck says: "To live so generously and unselfishly that the prospect of personal death—the night of the ego, it might be called—looks and feels less important than the secure knowledge that one has built for a broader, longer future than any one ego could ever encompass." (In B. L. Neugarten, *Middle Age and Aging*. Chicago: University of Chicago Press, 1968, p. 91.)

**The Measure of My Days.** Florida Scott-Maxwell. New York: Alfred A. Knopf, 1968. 150p.; Paper. New York: Penguin Books, 1979. $2.95.

The spiritual journey of Florida Scott-Maxwell is here recorded in diary form, reminiscent of John Woollman's *Journal* and so many others. Less than complete, yet here is the woman, struggling with the eternal problems of truth, God, mankind—and breaking off to a flurry of baking in the kitchen lest the terror of eternal questions overwhelm her. But then back to them again, with some insights to share. Honest, self-probing, illuminating, she rises above herself and her words shine with wisdom.

**Aging.** Henri J. M. Nouwen and Walter J. Gaffney. Photographs by Ron P. Van den Bosch. Garden City, N.Y.: Doubleday & Company, 1974. 152p.; Paper $2.45.

Subtitled "The Fulfillment of Life," this volume of reflections and photographs depicts the loss of self and the social segregation that often is part of aging, and then moves to consider the chosen transcendence of the self and commitment to the society of needful people. The achievement of a compassionate approach to life is seen as one of the rewards of aging, as possessions lose their power to constrain and as power over others is released for the exercise of caring.

**Markings.** Dag Hammarskjold. New York: Alfred A. Knopf, 1964. 221p. $11.95; London: Faber & Faber, 1966. $4.95.

A deeply personal and at times religious grouping of poems, essays, and sometimes simply sentences that reflect Hammarskjold's intense journey through life. Reflections with humor, joy, sadness, and a sense of reality that lead us to a truer sense of spiritual well-being.

**Death: The Final Stage of Growth.** Elisabeth Kübler-Ross. Englewood Cliffs, N.J.: Prentice-Hall, 1975. 192p. $2.95.

For Dr. Kübler-Ross, dying is an extraordinary act that involves the ultimate realities of life for the dying person and may do so for those close to him. Those in medical and nursing care are seen as needing to interfere as little as possible with these spiritual awarenesses in moments of passage.

BRA 14540

**The Irrational Season.** Madeleine L'Engle. New York: Seabury Press, 1977. 215p.

A woman's exploration of her life in terms of the people she has been: mother, wife, grandmother, and working woman. What is love and life and death and God? L'Engle says "The most difficult thing to let go is myself," and reflects that strangely "I come to be only as I lose myself." The experience of transcendence is as gradual as her maturing and as natural.

RD 10216

**Love and Will.** Rollo May. New York: W. W. Norton, 1969. 352p.; Paper. New York: Dell Publishing Company/Delta Books, 1973.

In his deep analysis of love in the human experience, May identifies a form of love that is a prerequisite of ego transcendence—a love that is not an egocentric assertion of one's subjective whims but rather an unselfish, giving love.

**A Gift from the Sea.** Anne Morrow Lindbergh. New York: Random House/Pantheon Books, 1955. 127p. $1.95; Large Type. New York: Franklin Watts, 1955. 128p.

The reflections here on married love at midlife crisis set a model of delicacy and honest probing for all reflection on life transitions and preparations. Of such sensitive self-assessment in the light of human experience is the path to both body and ego transcendence composed.

**The Search for Meaning.** Richard F. Hettlinger in collaboration with Grace Worth. Self-Discovery through the Humanities Series. Washington, D.C.: Senior Center Humanities Program, National Council on Aging, 1980. 230p. Large Type. Not for sale; Available on loan only to senior adult groups for discussion.

Brief selections from excellent literature, grouped around such topics as Personal Relationships, One with Nature, Truth in the Unseen, Accepting the Inevitable, and Creating Meaning: Sacrifice and Service. Designed for small group discussion, which can be arranged through the Senior Center Program, either locally or through information obtainable from the National Council on Aging.

Cassette format available from the National Council on Aging.

**A New Kind of Country.** Dorothy Gilman. Garden City, N.Y.: Doubleday & Co., 1978. 125p.; Large Type. Boston: G. K. Hall, 1979. $9.50.

Dorothy Gilman, writer, recounts her voyage of discovery into herself, which was the goal of her move from bustling suburban New York to rural Nova Scotia on the ocean. Here she records the steps of divesting herself of past and future to live in the Now, and of the doubts that gave moments of loneliness and alienation, of meeting small challenges in a new way of life, and of the gradual appearance of a sturdy new "personhood" with the inner security to be flexible and to be responsive to others.

RC 12702

**Learn to Grow Old.** Paul Tournier. New York: Harper & Row, 1973. 256p. $11.95.

In our lifetime and in our western society, Tournier sees the later years concerned with the relinquishment of power and the cultivation of the spirit. A sensitive, philosophic exploration of the possibilities of the human spirit. The role of faith is explored in one of the later chapters.

**A Time to Love, A Time to Die.** Prince Leopold Loewenstein. New York: Doubleday/Pyramid Publications, 1971. 276p.

A spiritual orientation to the acceptance of the death of a much-loved wife.

**Celebrations of Life.** René Dubos. New York: McGraw-Hill, 1981. 260p. $12.95.

Discusses the human condition and the process by which man became human. Readable, thought-provoking. Lucid and felicitous style.

*Creative Literature*

**"Certain Distant Sins."** Joanne Greenberg. In her *High Crimes and Misdemeanors*, pp. 66-97. New York: Holt, Rinehart and Winston, 1980. 228p. $9.95; Paper. New York: Avon Books, 1981. $2.95.

Aunt Bessie stops believing in God and celebrating the Jewish holidays and rituals. Then she stops believing in germs, banks, and electricity. When she can no longer believe in gravity, she must float through the house in tears. The crisis of faith for this 56-year-old woman makes a fascinating discussion-starter.

In the same collection is another fascinating story about spiritual identity. In "The Jaws of the Dog," Miriam's two elderly aunts, Rose and Gusta, have refused to move from the "rapidly decaying" old neighborhood. They live in constant fear of robbery, rape, and other violence. Miriam, with the help of a comparative religion professor, structures mystical rites and objects for them to use during their "crisis of faith." When they begin to believe in universal forces again, they drop their fears and are able to renew their lives outside the fortress of their home.

# PERSPECTIVE BUILDING

One of the unique contributions of older adults to the circle of friends and family, and perhaps to society at large, is the capacity for the long view and the broad perspective. Family history and traditions and the establishment and strengthening of old customs are meaningful in later years. Life review on the broad scale responds to the historical recounting of our own times and of the times of all humanity. The meaning of the human family emerges more strongly, and even the geological backgrounds of the planet earth come to provide perspective on our own lives.

Readings in this area reach broadly into all subjects. Selections here are merely suggestive of the kinds of readings which may provide intensive interest and satisfaction in the process of "putting it all together."

**The Ascent of Man.** Jacob Bronowski. Boston: Little, Brown, 1974. 448p. $24.95; Paper $14.95.

A scientific and intellectual history from the first fossil evidence of man to his twenty-first century commitment to knowledge. Thirteen essays on the development of science, drawn from the BBC television series, provide a framework for understanding the current explosion of scientific knowledge. Superbly illustrated.

RD 07462

**Civilisation: A Personal View.** Kenneth Clark. New York: Harper & Row, 1970. 359p. $25.00; Paper $10.95.

A history of Western Europe from the fall of Rome to the present, with its focus on the arts that have been fundamental to European civilization wherever it has spread. Drawn from the BBC television series, and well illustrated from that series.

TB 03737

**Connections.** James Burke. Boston: Little, Brown, 1978. 304p. $19.95; Paper 1980. $10.95.

Burke, a scientist, traces the historic roots of eight major technological inventions of our era: the computer, the production line, telecommunications, the airplane, the atomic bomb, plastics, the guided rocket, and television. This book is a companion to the BBC television series and is well illustrated from that series.

RD 15557

**Cosmos.** Carl Sagan. New York: Random House, 1980. 365p. $19.95.

An introduction to the basic structure of the universe as it is understood today, together with fascinating glimpses into the evolution of the major concepts and discoveries. Sagan is director of the Laboratory for Planetary Studies at Cornell University and was involved in the Mariner, Viking, and Voyager expeditions. This space-oriented view of our cosmology provides an important perspective. The volume is magnificently illustrated with charts, photographs, and paintings that assist the novice reader in comprehending space and the universe. Drawn from the KCET television series that attracted an audience of 140 million.

RD 15976

**The Immense Journey.** Loren Eiseley. New York: Random House, 1957. 210p. $10.95; Paper $1.95.

A slender volume that powerfully imagines the evolutionary events that led to our natural world and molded the human species. Based on scientific data, and even now — with much newer data available — remains an authentic introduction to this area of knowledge.

BRA 15519; TB 01556

**The Lives of a Cell: Notes of a Biology Watcher.** Lewis Thomas. New York: Viking, 1974. 153p. $10.95; Paper. New York: Bantam Books, 1975. $2.75; Paper. New York: Penguin Books, 1978. $3.95.

Readable, informal essays on biological topics rooted in human values and social concerns. Wide diversity of topics (efficiency of termite societies, misplaced priorities in medical research, symbiosis) which nevertheless introduce a novice reader to the scope of concerns that medical research and cancer research now encompass. Delightful humor, penetrating wit.

BR 02911; RD 0844

**A Sand County Almanac.** Aldo Leopold. London: Oxford University Press, 1949. 226p. $4.95.

A famous naturalist and prose stylist describes his family's experiences on a sand farm in Wisconsin. Written in the last year of his life, the *Almanac* is a beautiful, heartwarming book merging aesthetic values with ecology, forestry, and game management, and is expressive of deep concern for humanity and nature.

**As I Remember Him.** Hans Zinsser. Boston: Little, Brown, 1940. 443p.; Magnolia, Miss.: Peter Smith Publisher, Inc., n.d. $8.25.

Zinsser, scientist, world traveler, and physician, treated life as a journey and here recounts his own life with gusto, modesty, and candor. The autobiography closes with the author's approaching death and reflects his mastery of death as of life. Simplicity, humor, and grandeur of thought mark this unusual book.

**Yankee from Olympus.** Catherine Drinker Bowen. Boston: Little, Brown, 1944. 475p.

This biography of Justice Holmes and his poet father and his sons offers insight into the Boston Brahmins, the worlds of law and letters, as well as the national issues developing from the middle of the nineteenth century into the early twentieth.

BRA 11578; TB 01595

**First Person America.** Ann Banks. New York: Alfred A. Knopf, 1980. 320p. $13.95; Paper. New York: Random House, 1981. $5.95.

Eighty life-history narratives, selected from some 10,000 recorded by the Federal Writers Project interviewers in the 1930s. These present "the way people make sense of their lives, the web of meaning and identity they weave for themselves." Granite workers in Vermont, farmers on the frontier, labor unionists, jazz musicians, immigrants, and a wide variety of others provide their reminiscences and their perspective building.

**First Generation: In the Words of Twentieth Century American Immigrants.** June Namias. New York: Beacon Press/Harper Brothers, 1978. 224p. $12.95; Paper $5.95.

Panorama of immigration in the twentieth century through this collection of 31 interviews with American immigrants from all parts of the world, who came to seek work, refuge from political persecution, and educational opportunity. These are the roots for many of the older generation and these stories will stimulate perspective building. Similarly, Avis Carlson's *Small World, Long Gone* (Chicago: Chicago Review Press, 1977) recounts the roots in southern Kansas of Avis Carlson's family of Halls and Dungans, who had "bone-deep integrity, reading and arguing — or singing and laughing"; her families left her a significant heritage.

**Hidden Survivors: Portraits of Poor Jews in America.** Thomas J. Cottle. Englewood Cliffs, N.J.: Prentice-Hall, 1980. 190p. $9.95.

Survivors indeed! These dozen portraits construct a credible picture of the older Jewish urban poor in the United States, in their own familiar idiom and human warmth. The universal needs of older people for housing, love of friends and family, and life review are shown here in the lives of a handful of people important only for their humanity, their representativeness, and their capacity to express it for our understanding.

A similar resource is Barbara C. Myerhoff's *Number Our Days* (New York: Dutton, 1979. RD 13649) which offers reminiscence of roots in Jewish life in Europe, as reported by a group of elderly in the Aliyah Senior Citizens Center in Los Angeles. Warm, bitter, rich memories came from her meetings with the group on "Living History."

**The View in Winter: Reflections on Old Age.** Ronald Blythe. New York: Harcourt, Brace, Jovanovich, 1979. 288p. $12.95; Paper. New York: Penguin Books, 1980. $4.95.

A British humanist explores the world of aging in the vast reaches of the human experience in the small English village of "Akenfield." Viewed in the broad perspective of British life across the centuries, this rich store of vignettes of people is supported with a treasury of quoted verse that penetrates the experience of aging. Here is a rich perspective on aging itself. For leisurely, reflective reading.

RD 14013

More academic in style but interesting for its tracing of the roots of our ambiguity in attitude toward aging is W. Andrew Achenbaum's *Old Age in the New Land: The American Experience since 1790* (Baltimore: Johns Hopkins University Press, 1979).

**Human Options: An Autobiographical Notebook.** Norman Cousins. New York: W. W. Norton & Company, 1981. 224p. $9.95.

Norman Cousins, for years the editor of the *Saturday Review*, here shares from the years of writing and from recent experience, perspectives on a lifetime of sensitive awareness of the human scene. Perhaps his outstanding perception here is that there *are* human options, that alternatives do exist for mankind, that despair is not the only choice. World order, valuing human life, freedom in a democracy are some of his key concepts. "War is an invention of the human mind. The human mind can invent peace." "The main test before us involves our will to change rather than our ability to change." "Nothing is more powerful than an individual acting out of his conscience, thus helping to bring the collective conscience to life."

**American Journey: Traveling with Toqueville in Search of Democracy in America.** Richard Reeves. New York: Simon & Schuster, 1982. 399p. $15.95.

Recapitulates de Toqueville's early nineteenth century journey with a focus on how democracy is thriving. Does not have a strong single theme, but stimulates reflection.

**America in Search of Itself: The Making of the President, 1956-1980.** Theodore H. White. New York: Harper & Row, 1982. 456p. $15.95.

An account of 24 years of the passage of power, presented by a social critic saddened by inflation, declining American power abroad, and lost causes such as affirmative action for women and ethnic groups. Viewing ideals betrayed, principles abandoned, White protests the rise of alien, hostile forces in our country. The men and women, the issues, the scenes and controversies of these 40 years stand clearly before us.

## Creative Literature

**Angle of Repose.** Wallace Stegner. Garden City, N.Y.: Doubleday, 1971. 569p. $10.00; Paper. New York: Fawcett Book Group, 1979. $2.95.

A retired history professor and prize-winning author, Lyman Ward is living in his grandmother's cottage and tracing his family's history. We read that history as he uncovers it and writes about it. Confined to a wheelchair after an amputation, Lyman is a strong, independent, and interesting man trying to put his life into perspective.

BR 14974; RC 15186

**"Rabbi Ben Ezra."** Robert Browning.

Browning has a very optimistic perspective on aging in his famous poem which opens "Grow old along with me!/The best is yet to be."

Henry Wadsworth Longfellow is equally uplifting in his poem "Mezzo Cammin" in which the poet stops midway through life (the title's meaning) to put his life in perspective, looking both forward and back.

## Role of Tradition in Change

**"The Little Shoemakers."** Isaac Bashevis Singer. In his *Gimpel the Fool and Other Stories*, pp. 79-104. New York: Farrar, Straus and Giroux, 1957. 205p. $9.95; Paper. New York: Avon Books, 1957. $1.95.

Abba Shuster, master shoemaker in rural Poland, watches the emigration of his sons — one by one — to America and a new life. When the Nazi invasion forces Abba to leave his traditional home and ways to join his sons in America, his desolation is complete. Although Gimpel, the oldest, owns and operates a shoe factory, it is not until Abba discovers his old shoemaking tools that he is restored to full life. His sons, sharing his joy, celebrate in the traditional Judaic customs and make a specialty of Abba's handmade shoes. Tradition has found continuity in a new mode in a new home.

**"The Tree."** Noel Williard. *Short Story International* 3(14):77-89, June 1979.

When the government of New Zealand decides to remove the old metai tree to build sewers, the three community elders are upset. The modern bulldozers and saws cannot destroy it, but the elders decide to fell it by traditional methods to show their respect for the tree.

**The Last of My Solid Gold Watches.** Tennessee Williams. In *The Best One Act Plays of 1942*, pp. 1-15. Edited by Margaret Mayorya. New York: Dodd, Mead and Co., 1943.

Massive, dignified, 78-year-old "Mistuh Charlie" is a sales representative for the Cosmopolitan Shoe Company. An exemplary one at that—he has received fifteen solid gold watches as best salesman of the year during his 46 years selling in that territory. He tries to impress Bob Harper, a 35-year-old salesman, with his past but neither he nor the old hotel bellman care about Charlie's career. He exclaims: "I belong to tradition. I am a legend." The reader shares in his realization that those legendary days are nearly over.

RC 15738

**The Mary Celeste Move.** Frank Herbert. In *Eco-Fiction*. Edited by John Stadler. New York: Pocket Books, 1971. 211p. $1.95.

In 1998, Martin Fisk is en route to the Pentagon to report on a troubling new phenomenon—older people are moving in unusually high numbers to unlikely places. It seems that the high speed cars and 300 mph limits do not fit the lifestyle of people accustomed to a weekend leisurely drive. Once on the freeways, the drivers are unable to cope. As soon as possible, they leave the expressway, sell their cars, and settle down wherever they happen to be.

**Cry the Beloved Country.** Alan Paton. New York: Scribner, 1961. 283p. $15.00; Paper $3.95.

Although this lyrically beautiful novel is about the results of a native's murder of a rich white man in South Africa, a strong subplot concentrates on Stephen Kumalo, an old black parson, an Umfundisi in a rural village. He is called to the big city of Johannesburg to find his sister and discovers that his son Absalom has just committed murder. Kumalo's dilemma and the questions of justice and compassion in Johannesburg radicalize him and cause him to reconsider some of the traditional ways of his village.

BR 01948; TB 01918; Film. British Lion Films, 1951.

**"Everyday Use."** Alice Walker. In her *In Love and Trouble*, pp. 47-59. New York: Harcourt, Brace, Jovanovich, 1974; In *Black-Eyed Susans: Classic Stories by and about Black Women*, pp. 78-89. Edited by Mary Washington. New York: Doubleday, 1975. 200p. $3.95.

An older woman and her youngest daughter, Maggie, eagerly await the visit of Dee, the older child who is a success in the city. What a shock when Dee appears in African dress and hairstyle. Even her name is changed: she demands that they call her Wangero Leewanika Kemanjo. Her family's old-fashioned, rural ways used to dismay her, but now she is interested in everything, especially some "artistic" objects she wants to take back to the city. She claims a butter churn and some quilts, including two which were made for Maggie. When the mother-narrator refuses, Dee tells her that she doesn't understand her heritage and that she should change to fit the new day which has arrived for blacks.

RD 06927

**"Strong Horse Tea."** Alice Walker. In *Stories of the Modern South*, pp. 371-78. Edited by Ben Forkner and Patrick Samway. New York: Bantam Books, 1977. $2.65; New York: Penguin Books, 1981. $4.95.

Rannie Toomer is waiting for the black doctor to come and cure her ill child. Finally she listens to Sarah, the old healer's advice and tries an old folk remedy in a desperate attempt to save Snook's life. But it is too late.

## STAYING IN THE MAINSTREAM

The tasks of aging, many-faceted, are spread for most of us over 20, 30, or more years. And with them life in the mainstream of family, neighborhood, community, and beyond continues. As one's role shifts, new patterns of exchange and communication must be found to maintain the capacity to function in this mainstream. "Keeping current" is a process that takes on new patterns as retirement and lessening family and community responsibilities change our sources of information and daily contact with people. We read local and national newspapers, magazines, and journals more avidly for things we may have missed hearing; we watch media for the new facts and ideas that in earlier years we might have heard debated in our workplace or market. We look for books that may bring us up to date on topics of either casual or central importance to us; Charles Panati's *Breakthroughs* is a good example. Keeping current provides a sound basis for intergenerational communication and for assuring that the older adult's wisdom and influence have relevance and meaning within the current context. Keeping current is a central part of staying in the mainstream.

Older adults involved in political or social action are in the mainstream. Participation in reform and change does as much as any form of activity to maintain vital meaning in life. Whether volunteering in support of community activities or taking action on behalf of important social issues, older adults are contributing influence and leadership to events in their time. A significant function for experienced and seasoned older adults in mainstream activity is that of the "elder statesman," the role model and counselor of younger leaders. Here the broad view and concern for long-term social interests are unique and needed contributions from the older adult.

Ageism is one social ill to which social and political action by older adults can bring some measure of reform. Organizations as militant as the Grey Panthers or as establishment as the American Association of Retired Persons have already shown their power in forcing attention to the needs of older adults. While avoiding the purely self-serving role, contingents of older adults in the fights for (or against) nuclear arms or abortion or any of a multitude of other current issues are happily integrated into the general social movements. Volunteerism in political parties and community causes requires the energy and insight of all informed people. This new perspective on the later years is a significant one.

**Breakthroughs: Astonishing Advances in Your Lifetime in Medicine, Science, and Technology.** Charles Panati. Boston: Houghton, Mifflin Co., 1980. 306p. $12.95; Paper. New York: Berkley Publishing Company, 1981. $3.25.

Physicist and science writer, Panati details the major breakthroughs in pain, cancer, heart disease, and other health matters; nutrition, biorhythms, genes and reproduction; sleep, aging; weather, structure of the universe; electronics, space travel. Highly popularized, brief presentations reflective of *Woman's Day* and *Readers Digest*, for which Panati regularly writes.

**You Are Never Too Old to Learn.** Wilbur Cross and Carol Florio. New York: McGraw-Hill, 1978. 226p. $5.50.

Opens the door to learning opportunities of all kinds that keep one current and in the mainstream of thinking and knowledge. Useful lists of learning programs.

**How to Read a Book.** Rev. ed. Mortimer J. Adler and Charles Van Doren. New York: Simon & Schuster, 1972. 426p. $5.95.

The chapter on inspectional reading will well repay those eager to improve skills in "keeping current." Cut in half or less the time you spend with books and journals at the library shelves catching up on a variety of topics.

## POLITICAL AND SOCIAL ACTION

**The Grey Lobby.** Henry J. Pratt. Chicago: University of Chicago Press, 1977. 250p. $17.00; Paper 1980. $5.95.

History and analysis of how older adults achieved high political visibility in the 1960s and 1970s. Role of organizations and special interest groups within a coordinated plan. Picture of the colorful personalities and strong passions involved.

**Maggie Kuhn on Aging.** Margaret E. Kuhn. Philadelphia: Westminster Press, 1977. 140p. $3.95.

Kuhn, an outspoken leader of older Americans, founded Grey Panthers in 1972. Its goals are the liberation of older Americans from "paternalism and oppression with which society keeps us powerless." On behalf of an ecumenical group that develops Christian education, Maggie Kuhn has written this book on aging.

**"Gray Power."** Rebecca Blalock. In *Saturday Evening Post*, 251 (March 1979).

Maggie Kuhn and the purpose of her organization, the Grey Panthers.

**The Rights of Older Persons: An American Civil Liberties Union Handbook.** Robert N. Brown and others. New York: Avon Books, 1979. 434p. $2.50.

Covers legal rights in Social Security, SSI, pension laws, age discrimination in employment, Medicare and Medicaid, tax benefits, right to refuse medical treatment, and many other topics. Question and Answer format.

**Senior Power: Growing Old Rebelliously.** Paul Kleyman. San Francisco: Glide Publications, 1974. 177p.

History of a group of seniors at San Francisco's Glide Memorial Methodist Church, their activities and influence in political decisions. This book is a challenge to the ageist political and social status quo in America.

Mi-BPH (MSL-4092) RM

**Elders in Rebellion: A Guide to Senior Activism.** Louis M. Cottin. Garden City, NY: Doubleday/Anchor Press, 1979. 224p. $8.95.

Brief, tub-thumping chapters focus on some 18 issues which Cottin, author of the syndicated *Newsday* column, "Growing Older," sees as focus points for civic action by older adults. From "image" and status, through health, nursing care, income, and housing, to the use of leisure and public effectiveness for senior groups, Cottin points out the facts, problems, and alternatives for action which he and his retired wife have explored. His two major themes, "Seniors are getting a bad deal" and "Nothing is too good for older Americans," provide an accurate guide to the mood of this call to action.

**Rehabilitating America: Toward Independence for Disabled and Elderly People.** Frank Bowe. New York: Harper & Row, 1980. 203p. $11.95.

Bowe contends that a major financial saving could be made if the federal government would adequately fund programs in special education, rehabilitation, and barrier removal to give the disabled and elderly greater independence. Political activists among the elderly will find the rationale congenial. Bowe sees the enabling of the disabled as having a significant impact on unemployment, welfare, and tax problems of the country.

RD 15566

**Old Folks at Home.** Alvin Rabushka and Bruce Jacobs. New York: Free Press, 1980. 202p. $10.95.

Concluding from national survey data that most older adults are homeowners in reasonably good health (and *not* helpless, frail, poor, ill-housed), the authors propose that this new stereotype of the elderly be used to change government policy, removing earning limits on Social Security, removing minimum wage laws for the elderly, developing community and personal security programs to replace national programs. Timely, well written, with a clear viewpoint on an important issue.

**Crime Prevention Handbook for Senior Citizens.** Julie Edgerton. Kansas City, Mo.: Midwest Research Institute, 1977. 53p. $2.50.

A handbook describing how one can become a victim of crime and what practical things can be done to prevent victimization by burglary, robbery, larceny, or fraud.

**Consumer Complaint Guide.** Joseph Rosenbloom. 8th ed. New York: Macmillan, 1981. 442p. $12.50; Paper 1979. $5.95.

The first few pages of the book are devoted to basic information about consumer rights, guarantees, warranties, and how to go about making a complaint. Then follows a classified directory of product and service companies, with addresses and names of officials to whom complaints should be addressed.

**The Older American's Handbook: Practical Information and Help on ... for Older Americans.** Craig and Peter Norback. New York: VanNostrand Reinhold Company, 1977. 311p. $3.95.

Chapter 15 on housing lists addresses of state offices of the Farmers Home Administration, U.S. Housing and Urban Development, housing finance and development agencies, and public housing agencies for each state. Other chapters have comparable information on a diversity of subjects.

**The Handbook of Human Services for Older People.** Edited by Monica Bychowski Holmes and Douglas Holmes. New York: Human Sciences Press, 1979. 300p. $24.95.

A welcome guide to the agencies and services in each of eight major areas of service to older adults. Less a "consumer's guide" than a map to the proliferating agencies for service providers. The knowledgeable consumer, however, will find scanning of these resources enlightening. Each area is described for its topic generally, the federal legislation relevant, service categories, and delivery mechanisms. Useful bibliographies.

# SOURCES FOR FURTHER READING
of Creative Literature on Aging

## OTHER BIBLIOGRAPHIES OF IMAGINATIVE LITERATURE ON AGING

Kellam, Constance E. *A Literary Bibliography on Aging.* New York: Council on Social Work Education, 1968.

Moss, Walter G. *Humanistic Perspectives on Aging: An Annotated Bibliography and Essay.* Ann Arbor, Mich.: Institute of Gerontology, 1976.

National Retired Teachers Association and American Association of Retired Persons. *Learning about Aging.* Chicago: American Library Association, 1981.

Sohngen, Mary. "The Experience of Old Age as Depicted in Contemporary Novels." *The Gerontologist* 17(1):70-78, 1977.

## ANTHOLOGIES OF CREATIVE LITERATURE ON AGING

Alvarez, Ronald A. F., and Susan C. Kline, eds. *Images of Aging in Literature.* 3rd ed. Washington, D.C.: National Council on the Aging, 1978.

Larrain, Virginia. *Timeless Voices: A Poetry Anthology Celebrating the Fulfillment of Age.* Millbrae, Calif.: Celestial Arts, 1978.

Lyell, Ruth Granetz, ed. *Middle Age, Old Age: Short Stories, Poems, Plays, and Essays on Aging.* New York: Harcourt, Brace, Jovanovich, 1980.

Maclay, Elise. *Green Winter: Celebrations of Old Age.* New York: Readers' Digest Press, 1977.

Schulman, L. M., ed. *Autumn Light: Illuminations of Age.* New York: Thomas Y. Crowell, 1978.

## ANTHOLOGIES ON RELATED TOPICS

Adler, Charles S. et al. *We Are but a Moment's Sunlight: Understanding Death.* New York: Pocket Books, 1976.

Hamalian, Linda, and Leo Hamalian. *Solo: Women on Women Alone.* New York: Dell Publishing Co., 1977.

Hamalian, Leo, and Frederick R. Karl. *The Fourth World: The Imprisoned, the Poor, the Sick, the Elderly, and the Underaged in America.* New York: Dell Publishing Co., 1976.

Moffat, Mary Jane. *In the Midst of Winter: Selections from the Literature of Mourning.* New York: Vintage Books, 1982.

O'Rourke, William. *On the Job: Fiction about Work.* New York: Vintage Books, 1977.

# AUTHOR-TITLE INDEX

# SUBJECT INDEX